Beautifully You

Natalie P Epps

30 DAYS OF INVITATIONS TO ENCOUNTER
THE HOLY SPIRIT

Beautifully You

BY NATALIE EPPS

Copyright © 2017 Natalie Epps

All rights reserved. No parts of this book may be reproduced in any form, without permission from the author, except by reviewers, who may quote brief passages in a review.

References:
Scripture quotations unless otherwise indicated are from the *English Standard Version Bible*, copyright 2001 by Crossway, a publishing ministry of Good News Publishers. Used by permission. All rights reserved.

Scripture quotations marked TPT are from *The Pslams: Poetry on Fire*, The Passion Translation, copyright 2014. Used by permission of BroadStreet Publishing Group, LLC, Racine, Wisconsin, USA. All rights reserved.

All quotes in interior artwork are paraphrased scripture and not necessarily directly quoted from any specific translation

Day 19: Kris Vallotton, "The Power of Belonging", Bethel Church, Redding California
Day19: Berne Brown, "The Power of Vulnerability"

Cover art by: Christian Smith
Interior artwork by: Andrew Clark
Back cover photography by: Kismet Visuals and Co.
Publish by: CreateSpace

NatalieEpps.com

ISBN-10: 1978380844
ISBN-13: 978-1978380844

Dedication

To my incredible husband, Jonah, my resilient daughters, and the scores of family and friends who enabled me through love to live and feel each moment of this journey. You are gold.

Contents

Day 1: Beautifully you	Pg. 2
Day 2: Belonging	Pg. 5
Day 3: Faith that pleases God	Pg. 8
Day 4: Running with endurance	Pg. 10
Day 5: Honey I shrunk my dreams	Pg. 13
Day 6: Peace - the dove or the dragon	Pg. 16
Day 7: There goes grace	Pg. 19
Day 8: Artifacts	Pg. 22
Day 9: Joy comes in the mourning	Pg. 26
Day 10: The tenderizer	Pg. 29
Day 11: Leading by living	Pg. 32
Day 12: Song birds	Pg. 36
Day 13: Staying still when you want to run	Pg. 39
Day 14: Responsibility to heal	Pg. 42
Day 15: Free to fail	Pg. 45
Day 16: Songs for your season	Pg. 49
Day 17: Promises you shouldn't keep	Pg. 52
Day 18: Your seat at the table	Pg. 55
Day 19: Breaking Shame	Pg. 59
Day 20: Imposter	Pg. 62
Day 21: In-between	Pg. 65
Day 22: Honoring your 'why	Pg. 68
Day 23: Lateral moves	Pg. 71
Day 24: Growing weeds	Pg. 74
Day 25: A new name	Pg. 77
Day 26: Staying thankful	Pg. 80
Day 27: Timeless	Pg. 83
Day 28: Coats in the summer	Pg. 86
Day 29: The "L" word	Pg. 89
Day 30: An inside job	Pg. 92

Preface

Why *Beautifully You*? In 2012, one month prior to my wedding, I lost my father to cancer. Three years later, in 2015, I lost the function of one side of my face to a brain tumor. Unable to love what I saw in my reflection, I sat down to write this devotional. What was originally intended to be 30 words for 30 days of what makes a woman "beautifully her", became a flood of a collection of stories of intense encounters with the Lord, and how they have changed me. It was through the recollection of these stories that I realized that it was not what was in the mirror, but the pieces of my heart that make me, "beautifully me". And what I believe make you, *Beautifully You*. I pray that as you read, you find yourself in these pages, and that as you do, you would be wrecked by the awesome love of a relentless Go

"You are altogether beautiful, my darling; there is no flaw in you"

Day 1: Beautifully You

Have you ever wanted to stand out and blend in all at the same time?

In 2015, I was diagnosed with an Acoustic Neuroma, a brain tumor that had wrapped its way around my balance, hearing and facial nerve and was pressing into my brain stem. Unfortunately, this kind of tumor generally grows silently over decades until it begins to impair its unknowing host. Blindsided by the diagnosis, my husband and I began to believe God for my total healing. And after a period of months, while still totally trusting in the Lord, I underwent a craniotomy in late 2015. Coming out of surgery I expected the recovery to be intense. However, what I didn't expect was that the right side of my face would be completely paralyzed; a side effect that I would discover in the following days was a rare side effect that came with no prognosis.

Today we've all heard at least two handfuls of messages on how we've been created uniquely by God. How no one else can offer this world what we can ... and it's true, but as the months progressed and my healing marched on at a snail's pace, I remember thinking a million times over how I'd love to be just like everyone else. I'd love to blink and smile. I had always loved being with and in front of people, but now I avoided public appearances like the plague and could hardly muster the courage to venture out past my living room. Regardless of my desires, I was anything but like everyone else.

Months before I remember telling my husband I felt like I was causing our family to miss out on the fun things in life. I would sit on social media and scroll through picture after picture of smiles. Posed smiles, candid smiles, kid smiles and more. I just wanted to be like the people I saw. My husband, Jonah, had an entirely different take. He explained how today people are inundated by hundreds of other images daily of people who look exactly like everyone else. He wasn't saying in "looks" necessarily, but in life. He encouraged me that where other things blended into the background I stood out because I had a story and it was worth stopping to hear. To be honest with you, I had never thought of my journey in that way.

1 Peter 4:10-11 says, "As each has received a special gift, employ it in serving one another as good stewards of the manifold grace of God. Whoever speaks, is to do so as one who is speaking the utterances of God; whoever serves is to do so as one who is serving by the strength which God supplies; so that in all things God may be glorified through Jesus Christ, to whom belongs the glory and dominion forever and ever. Amen." ESV

Regardless of the challenges or thoughts of inability in our lives, the Word says that we have been given specific gifts from God, and that we are to use them "in serving one another".

What would it look like if instead of hiding behind who we believed we were not, we stood confidently in who we know that we are. I believe that in this day the Lord is calling us out of our hiding places as women, and simply asking us to be who we are good at.

Whether it's worship or art, speaking or listening, organizing or teaching, being an employee or a fulltime mom at home, we were each given gifts at the beginning of time. Gifts that were determined before unplanned failures or sicknesses. Gifts that were distributed before the world could disqualify us. Gifts that God is asking us today to "serve one another" with.

My prayer for you today is that you would begin to let confidence rise in you, and begin chipping away at all the thoughts that disqualify you from running after your passions. I pray that in this moment you would stop seeing who you are not, and get a glimpse of who you are. And that you would decide now to take one step closer to the woman Christ created you to be, and one step away from the woman the world shaped you in to. And that you would find yourself being free to be who you are good at, today!

"But I know the way back home"

Day 2: Belonging

Have you ever been surrounded with people and all alone at the same time?

About two years ago, my husband and I were faced with a hard decision. The church we had met in and had been a part of for over a decade was going through an intense time of transition. And in the season, we had a choice to make; should we stay or should we go? It was a decision that was ultimately made through lots of prayer and lots and lots of tears. In the end, we knew the Holy Spirit was moving us on. And through a season of waiting before the Lord and keeping our hearts soft, we were led very supernaturally to a new church home.

Now I am a "belonger". I love belonging. The body I had been a part of previously wasn't this mega church of thousands, it was more like 70 people that I lived week in and week out with, celebrated holidays with ... this was a family. While I still had several of my most important relationships in tact after our departure, it didn't detract from the fact that I felt very alone.

I am the type of person that when I'm in, I am all in. And I suddenly found myself in this new place I knew I was supposed to be, trying to make myself belong. It was in months of coming to the Lord that He began to show me how purposeful this season of loneliness was. I hadn't done anything wrong and I wasn't "weird", but I was definitely prone to imbalanced and unhealthy loyalties, and God in His goodness was working it out of me.

One morning spending time with the Lord I was up early listening to some music. I was listening to a song I had heard many times before,

"Where I Belong" by Cory Asbury. But this time I caught a phrase that I hadn't quite heard the same before. The song says, "I finally found where I belong, I finally found where I belong, in your presence". In my worship, I laughed out loud. Man, oh man, why was it so hard to realize that I didn't need physically to belong to a house or people? (though community is essential and I would shrivel up and die without it) The only place I really needed to belong was in His presence... and I already did. I had a home address the entire time: The address of the throne room of the Lord.

Psalm 5:7 says, "But I know the way back home, and I know that you will welcome me into your house. For I am covered by your covenant of mercy and love. So, I come to your sanctuary with deepest awe to bow in worship and adore you." TPT

The older we get the more we see change in our lives. And regardless if it is change that we perceive as good or bad, what matters the most is that through the change we remember that the home address of our souls is in the presence of the Lord. While I believe fully in putting roots down in a local body, I also want to share with you what I have found out the hard way, and that is that we'll always feel like wanderers and outcasts if the real longing in our belonging is not satisfied first within the Heart of the Lord.

Today I want to pray for those of you reading this who like me may be going through a season of "longing" in your desire to belong. I want to encourage you that when you feel alone in a sea of people, that God is lasered on you. His desire is in time, to bring you into beautiful community as you learn your place at the feet of our God. Be encouraged and filled with joy today because I assure you that you are on the heart of the Father. And though I know that loneliness can be a hard place, I can also tell you that the Lord has gone before you and provided a soft, peaceful, welcoming place for you. And today I encourage you to enter

> *"Without faith it is impossible to please God"*

Day 3: faith that pleases God

Have you ever wondered what it takes to please God?

I remember the day my dad passed away. He died of cancer when I was 28, just 6 weeks before my wedding. What I learned about who God is and who He became personally to me during that time has shaped so much of who I am today.

I was with him along with my mom and siblings when he went. We didn't think he was going, but once we were all there it happened very quickly. After he passed, a doctor shepherded us into a small room where we could be alone and take some time consoling one another. When we stepped out of the room, we were met by a hallway full of loved ones.

So many people had come to see him. So many people loved him. Those moments play back like slow motion in my mind. It was like a movie where you can see everyone crying and hugging but the audio has been cut out. I remember Jonah moving down the hall towards where I stood and taking ahold of me. I didn't know what to say. This healing I had stood for and believed for had slipped through my fingers, and now my dad was in eternity. Without missing a beat Jonah pulled me close and said, "the Word says that without faith it's impossible to please God; and God is so pleased with you".

So many times we base our right standing with God and His approval of us by our circumstances, when the truth is that He's only asked us to believe in His ability to be Lord. God wasn't judging my faith that day by whether my dad lived or died, but rather He was looking and waiting to see if even in a moment of deep disappointment I would choose Him.

He isn't judging us based on our "passes" and "fails", but far more than that He's inviting us into the chance to see His goodness in our lives in all seasons. The truth of the matter is that my Dad is in Heaven. He's now and for all eternity worshipping before the Father. My faith that day wasn't about the success of my prayer (though I know all things are possible), as much as it was about the response of my heart. You see, believing God doesn't come without risks. In fact, if you're reading this then I know that you know by experience that giving God your "yes" means opening yourself up to both victories and failures. But our promise remains that when life brings us trouble that we can maintain an attitude of victory because Christ has already overcome it all.

My prayer for you today is that you wouldn't get tripped up by the circumstances of life. I pray that you wouldn't allow them, whether small or large, to cast a shadow on who you believe God is, or tangle up the truth that our Heavenly Dad is actually very pleased with you. Like the father of the possessed boy, sometimes the most faith filled prayer you can pray is "I believe You, but help my unbelief". So, today I declare truth over you. I declare that God isn't daunted by your humanity ... but instead He is pleased with you and by you. And that as you read these words you would feel Him standing by eagerly waiting for the invitation to invade your day.

"Run with endurance the race that is set before us"

Day 4: Running with endurance

There are two types of people in this world. Those who like running, and everyone else.

I know a lot of people strongly dislike it, but I have always loved to run. It's always been a way for me to clear my mind and recharge my body.

I vividly remember in school the first week of track practice always being the most humorous. Track isn't something you have to "try out" for. You just show up and whoever is brave or crazy enough to stick it out makes the team. You would always start with a gymnasium of a hundred kids ... And four days later you'd have 20.

When I was in junior high my coach at the time was this short and fiery lady. She would yell at us all the way around the track and jump up and down as we crossed the finish line. We were at the age where the coaches would collaborate and try us at different distances. Unfortunately for me, I was born with zero foot speed, so the 100 and 200 quickly passed me by, leaving only the longer sprints and distances to try. I remember the first time my coaches timed me in the 400, aka the "race of death".

The 400 is not short enough to be a dead sprint, but not long enough for a real pace, it's square in the middle. The objective is to run as fast and hard as you can without dying 300 meters in. It's a calculated race that you'll only know if you've done it right as you turn the corner into your final 100 meters.

I remember coming down the final stretch of rubbery track and my coach staring at me with her head tilted sideways. I crossed the finish line certain that I was taking in my final breaths of life. Struggling to regain composure I walked over to her. She looked at me and said, "it's the craziest thing. You hit that last stretch and it's just like your legs grew." Now at 5'1 that's definitely a compliment. And while I was happy I'd done a good job, I was also nervous knowing I'd just adopted the hardest race as my own.

Watching latest summer's Olympics in Rio, I was reminded of how easy it is to be a spectator. Watching the runners sprint around the track I was reminded of the cries I would hear as I turned that final corner. "Run faster!", "You're almost there!" To the one watching it was easy to see that the race was nearly over. But to the individual running it seemed like the finish line crept millimeter by millimeter further away.

Hebrews 12:1 says, "Therefore, since we are surrounded by so great a cloud of witnesses, let us also lay aside every weight, and sin which clings so closely, and let us run with endurance the race that is set before us." ESV

Reflecting on the Olympics made me think of walking through physical healing. You sit, and wait and believe for the fullness of the physical manifestation of healing in your body. And though you would assume that as you began to see glimmers of healing the race would get easier. But the truth is that sometimes that's when it gets the hardest.

I'm sure today as you read this that you can call to mind a situation in your life where you've run a hard race. Maybe you're still running. You've turned the corner and now you're looking down the lane seeing the finish line coming slowly into focus. It's the feeling of "this is almost over" and "why is that line so far away" all at the same time.

And I believe just like in my story from Junior High track, that today that the Father is saying, "it's time to grow".

Today I want you to think on the race you are currently running.

I pray that in this moment God would elevate your eyes to see what others in the stands around you can see. That though your eyes may be blurry from the running, the finish line is within reach. Listen to the cloud of witnesses around you as the cheer you on to victory. I pray that in this moment, you would stretch your legs and instead of leaning back in doubt or exhaustion, that you lean in like never before.

I pray that as you lean in God would reveal and intensify the specific grace He has released to you for this moment, for this journey, for this race.

> *"The Word is a lamp to our feet, a light to our path"*

Day 5: Honey I shrunk my dreams

Have you ever been afraid to dream?

I have never had a problem "thinking big". I always thought that my life in one way or another would lead to something great. I credit a lot of that to my parents who saw all of my antics and never stopped me from trying. From the basketball team, to cheerleading, band, choir, chorale, theater and beyond... I wasn't good at all of them, and some of them I never even made the cut. But I always had this voice in me that said "just try", and I never had parents that stood in my way. I was far from Ms. Popular or Homecoming Queen, but I always felt like if I never stopped trying, that somewhere doors would open in one way or another ... and they generally did.

The last few years have challenged every one of my dreams. I always thought I would end up speaking in front of people in some fashion. It comes easy to me. I'm not nervous in the slightest of large crowds and actually draw energy from being in front of them.

Facial Paralysis changed that.

One day a little over a year ago I was recovering from my third surgery. I had hoped this would be the final leg of my journey. But instead, I sat in my living room hooked up to a bag of IV antibiotics trying to close yet another incision that wouldn't heal. I remember in that moment being pained by all the things I had so heavily leaned on as my strengths. It hurt so badly to think of what I would have to reduce my life to. I couldn't think any more about the things I had at one point wanted to do. And so, for a season I stopped dreaming.

Fast forward to early 2017, now healing from my fourth surgery. And while I was still contending with issues in my body I had begun to have feelings of hope that just maybe I would get better. Maybe I could still share with people the way I thought I once would. After all, now I had something to say. And that day, as I stood looking into the living room where I had sat before with despair, I heard the Lord say,

"don't shrink the size of your dreams because the season you're in feels small".

Wow.

How many of us are guilty of this? How many times have we knowingly or unknowingly diminished the dreams in our heart purely to find satisfaction in life? God has called us all to greatness. And He's given each of us paths and story lines of just what that looks like in our lives. I believe that so many times we abandon the dreams God has placed in us not because we don't want to see them come to pass, and not because we don't believe in them anymore, but because life turns our visions into pipe dreams. We convince ourselves that we were just young dreamers without a real grasp on how life worked and to be happy with where we are, we have to give them up and settle.

I believe that God is better than that. I don't know how He'll accomplish the dreams He's placed in my heart or yours. But as I've learned over the last two years, sometimes the biggest step you can make is the one where you put one foot in front of the other. A season can feel small, but it doesn't mean that it is.

What I want to tell you today, is don't define what's possible in the future, by measuring your dreams against who you are right now. I know it can hurt to stir up dreams. I know it can be painful to look back at the hopes you once held on to. But take courage, and allow the pain to remind you of the desire and passion you once had.

Maybe at this moment you cannot see any viable path to get there. But Psalms 119:105 says that when we cannot see our feet in front of us, that "the Word is a lamp to my feet, a light to my path". ESV

God desires to dream with us with and has given us irrevocable gifts and callings. And today I believe the Lord is speaking to your spirit and saying, "It's time to dream again".

Today I want to pray over your dreams. God, I thank you that you have created every person reading this to bring Heaven to Earth. I speak to those who have laid their dreams down, those who feel like they've had to let go. God, I ask that today you would begin to breathe again on these places in their heart. Quiet the fears and disappointments and remind them that You are the one who gives dreams and destiny, and release over them today the plans of Heaven. I declare clarity and direction, and that the windows of Heaven are open over them. I bind the lie that they have to compromise the dreams in their heart for the life they are living. Instead I declare that You are good, and able to do exceedingly abundantly above all that we can ask or think. I thank You, God, for the freedom to dream again, today.

"The peace of God will guard you"

Day 6: Peace – the dove or the dragon

Have you ever been in a moment where you needed peace less like a dove and more like a dragon?

I remember the night after my dad passed away. I had gone home to the house I lived in with my room mates. I was exhausted from the past 48 hours and it was all I could do to collapse on my bed. My tears and my emotions were exhausted. My body laid on the bed like a wet wool blanket; my heart so broken.

I laid there on my sheets, as my heart turned heavily towards my siblings, who had just lost their Father. Thinking of graduations to come, aisles to walk down and grandchildren yet to be born I opened my mouth to cry out for their hearts. I began to cry out for God to protect them in this incredibly emotional and vulnerable moment in time. Knowing that the morning to come would bring the sting of reality like a wave back over them. But that night as I began to speak, I instantly heard the voice of God probably louder and clearer than I have in my entire life.

He spoke and said, "No, stop praying, it's time to sleep". My heart was so wrung out that those words were like water to my tired soul. Unlike many, including myself, would assume, I didn't toss and turn that night ... instead I rolled over and immediately fell asleep.

The next morning, I was getting ready for my now husband, then fiancé, to pick me up and take me back to my family's house. I was sitting on the floor reading the Word and listening to music. As I was listening, I read Philippians 4:7,"And the peace of God, which surpasses all understanding, will guard your hearts and your minds in Christ Jesus." ESV. In that moment, I remember thinking of how desperately I needed the peace of God. But I was afraid that it wouldn't be enough.

This was territory unlike any other. I was so unsure of what emotion would come next or what the day would hold, that in my mind I needed something more than a flighty dove, I needed something to breathe fire on all the new and unwelcome thoughts that were careening their way towards my heart. I had always read that scripture in such a light and airy way, but in that moment, I was desperate for something more. And as those thoughts filled my mind I looked back at the scripture and saw something I hadn't seen before. God's peace was guarding me.

For some reason up until that point I had this flighty and skittish interpretation of the peace of God. I don't know about you, but when I think of a guard I don't think of some light and fluffy marshmallow puff standing at a gate. I imagine someone strong and intimidating, someone who has been trained for confrontation.

How many times have we done this? How many times have we sold ourselves short when it comes to picturing and embracing the peace of God? What I discovered in that moment was that when God declares that His peace will guard us there is absolutely nothing passive about it. He is strong and unwavering and is able to destroy the thoughts and feelings that come for our soul.

His peace is not timid or easily moved by the challenges in our life, ... because His Peace is a person. Peace is Jesus, and He is passionate about us.

Today I want to pray for the aggressive peace of God to barrel into your life. I pray that every area in your heart that is crying out for retaliation against thoughts of pain, anger, frustration or confusion, would be met by the Person of peace and that they would dissolve beneath the weight of His presence.

I declare over you that there is a guard well abled to stand at the thresh hold of your heart and, that the dove sitting on your shoulder would breathe fire. God, I pray over us as your daughters, that You would release to each of us a deeper and more intense revelation of just how powerful and overcoming your peace for each of us is, today.

> "There is a time for everything under heaven"

Day 7: There goes grace

Have you ever known that person who outstays their welcome? Has that person ever been you?

I have been pregnant twice in my life. And twice I've given birth, by cesarean, to two beautiful girls. Other than morning aka all the time, sickness, my pregnancies weren't bad. But just like any other woman, by the end I was DONE.

As I learned through my pregnancies, one of the markers a woman always has in the back of her head is this term, 'viability'. It's a term that pertains to the baby's ability to sustain life outside of the womb. Up until this age of viability the baby is entirely dependent on its mother. The baby cannot and would not survive if separated from the womb. Now, if you've ever been pregnant, then you know that there is nothing as sad as seeing 40 weeks come and go. And though we know babies come "when they're ready", once you get to about 42 weeks if you haven't given birth yet, the chances of a stillbirth can rise. Because while for 40(ish) weeks a baby needs its mother's body, there comes a point where they also need to separate. This separation is healthy, it's normal and it's necessary. The grace for both mom and baby begins to lift.

Ecclesiastes 3:1-8 says, For everything there is a season, and a time for every matter under heaven:
    2 a time to be born, and a time to die;
    a time to plant, and a time to pluck up what is planted;
    3 a time to kill, and a time to heal;
    a time to break down, and a time to build up;
    4 a time to weep, and a time to laugh;
    a time to mourn, and a time to dance;
    5 a time to cast away stones, and a time to gather stones together;
    a time to embrace, and a time to refrain from embracing;
    6 a time to seek, and a time to lose;
    a time to keep, and a time to cast away;
    7 a time to tear, and a time to sew;
    a time to keep silence, and a time to speak;
    8 a time to love, and a time to hate;
    a time for war, and a time for peace." ESV

Have you ever found yourself in the place where you felt the grace of God lifting off of a season of your life?

Let's use an example that not all, but a lot of us have been through. Leaving a church. Maybe you have been a part of this house for a long time. You helped plant it, you lead small groups, you planned outreaches and retreats ... these are your people. And then one day it stops flowing the way it did before. Now please understand I am not giving anyone an "out" just because they no longer like the music, the pastor's messages or skinny jeans (insert trigger). What I am talking about, is a moment where you realize that God's grace is lifting from that season and He is leading you on.

Change can be terrifying. And if you've been through enough of it, you know it's true. But what is worse than change is refusing to move when you feel God's grace shifting in a situation. Sure, you can fake it for a while, but you know as real as the words on this page, that when you step outside of God's grace, that's when things really get hard. It doesn't have to be a church. It can be anything, relationships, jobs, etc. You felt God's hand on it for a season, but then it begins to lift. It almost feels wrong to think about leaving or stopping, and unless God tells you to, don't! But what I am saying today is that there are some of us who know we are trying to outstay the grace of God in a situation in our lives. And today I want to say that is not a place you want to be.

Moving on can have such bad connotations. But the truth is that it doesn't have to be negative. It doesn't have to be traumatic. Sometimes it's just what God's doing. And the worst thing we can do is fail to recognize when a season is over. After all, if God is the one who created seasons in the natural, then why do we fail to recognize them in the spiritual? I believe it's because we enjoy being loyal. We like consistency, and change can be uncomfortable. But what I want you to see today is that there are new things the Lord is waiting to bring forth in your life, but to grab hold of it, you have to let go. And you can't stop there. Instead of lingering over the moments, and gazing off into the distance, recounting what 'was', begin to look with expectation to the future for where God 'is'.

> "And if we know that He hears us – we know that we have what we ask of Him"

Day 8: Artifacts

Has anybody ever accused you of being the nostalgic type? Perhaps you're self-professed as a keeper of all things "important"?

I remember once going home and my mom giving me a closet full of boxes to go through. I had kept everything from my adolescent years. From dried flowers and notes, to pictures and journals, I kept it all. As I've gotten older I've mostly become a minimalist. I've tried to create space in my life, and house, for all of the crayon scribbled treasures and special rocks that my girls bring home. But one thing I don't want to ever outgrow collecting, or become a minimalist at, is the collection of tangible testimonies of God's goodness in my life.

Several months back, I was listening to a podcast by Bill Johnson. I don't remember the exact subject he was speaking on, but part of his message was a story of when he was younger in ministry. He had just received some money for his birthday and really wanted to buy a rifle. Ultimately wisdom kicked in and he determined that paying the bills was probably a better use of his money than buying a gun. He shared how later that same week an older man in his congregation approached him and asked if he needed a rifle. To which he of course responded, "yes, yes I do". Now you know the end of the story. The man ended up taking Bill to his personal rifle collection and letting him pick out one as his own. Bill spoke about how that rifle stood in his collection over time as a physical sign of something that he could have purchased on his own, but in waiting and operating in obedience, God was able to truly give Bill a gift.

1 John 5:15 says, "And if we know that he hears us in whatever we ask, we know that we have the requests that we have asked of him." ESV

My pastor asked recently if my life was a book what chapter am I on? After a little thought, I decided that it would be called something like "Christmas Morning". I've come out of a tough season, but through this season I've gained very specific gifts from God as testimonies of His goodness.

One really simple story I can share was as I was on the journey of writing this devotional. Being a wife, mom and employee left me with very little time for something I felt God was leading me to do. Now I could have asked my husband to take the girls and give me space to write, but considering my time with them was already so limited I didn't feel like that was the right thing to do. After about a month of writing I was at a small group explaining to the women that I needed prayer for space to complete what was in my heart to do. One of the women praying for me told me she saw my boss just giving me time off that I could use to write. I thought, wow that would be incredible. I don't see it happening, but that would be awesome.

That was on a Wednesday night. Fast-forward to the following Monday morning. I sat down to my computer and began to open emails. I was quickly reminded that this week was employee appreciation week. There were balloons and food and cards and all the things to make showing up to work just a little more enjoyable. As I went through my emails I came across one from my areas leader. He was thanking us for all our hard work. He wrote how there were other things he could give us, but he wanted to give us the gift of time... he literally gave us a half day off of our choosing. Exactly what had been prayed.

Now I could have easily "made" time. I have along the way and there is nothing wrong or selfish about that. But I thought it was so cool how God wanted to step in and answer a very specific request. Not only was it a really cool testimony of provision, but also a reminder that He was the one urging me and releasing me to write. And even when it came down to the most natural thing, such as the clock, that God was all over it.

And I believe today God is re-inviting us to evaluate the requests we've made to Him and the ones we've withheld because they are technically within our ability to make happen. I know that He is looking and waiting for very real ways to step in and show us not only does He support us in our desires, but He delights in giving us the best gifts a father can give.

I have stories of so many things that through waiting on the Lord have added faith to my prayers. Not every answered prayer has been this huge Earth-shattering thing. But when we stop to ask for something simple, and it happens, what builds on the inside of us is this internal dialogue that my God is interested in every detail of my life. And today I want to stir you to remember the museum of "artifacts", stories and tangible gifts of God that He has given you throughout your life. What did those small or large things do for your faith? And have you stopped asking and looking for them?

Today I want to pray that your memory would call back the things you have stopped asking for. Maybe they are small things and maybe they are large, but today I release over you the inspiration to ask again. God, I thank you that you honor the words of your daughters. I call back lost things. I call forward things asked for and prayers given for others. I thank you that you are the God who hears us (1John5:14). So, today I declare a renewed determination to approach boldly Your throne of Grace. And to ask of our Father from whom all good and perfect gifts flow. And I declare today that You would fill the hallways of our lives with testimonies of your goodness.

> *"But joy comes in the morning"*

Day 9: Joy comes in the mourning

Have you ever tried to skip the mourning to get to your morning?

When my dad passed away several years ago from cancer I felt like my world was collapsing around me. I knew what God's word said about healing, and I believed it. And now here I was on the other side of my dad's death trying to figure out how to merge my mourning with the promises of God.

I remember one day in particular as I was praying/crying before the Lord. I just felt so much pain in my heart. I knew who God was, but experiencing what I had it was hard to do anything other than worship through the tears. I'll never forget that day laying on my bed prying (praying/crying). I saw this little bottle in my spirit. It was filled partially with water and partially with oil. In my vision, I was holding this little bottle and shaking it vigorously trying to get the water and oil to mix. But no matter how hard I shook, the two wouldn't come together. I became so frustrated that I finally threw the bottle to the ground. That's when through my vision the Holy Spirit spoke. He whispered and said, "the bottle is you". "The water is your mourning and the oil is your joy, and you're trying desperately to get them to mix. Stop trying to mask your sorrow. You don't have to worry about the mixture. Just pour the bottle out to me and let me take care of you".

That experience with the Lord changed me.

We're all familiar with Psalm 30:5 " Weeping may tarry for the night, but joy comes with the morning " ESV. It's a verse that we hear quoted time and time again when speaking of hard times. People read the scripture and encourage us to "hang on" because joy is coming. Now I don't want to discredit that, because it's true. God is always breaking through our night with his light, His joy. But today what I want to propose is that we don't have to skip the night. That joy not only comes in the morning, but if we'll let it, joy can come in the mourning.

How many times in life have we been guilty of so desperately trying to get past the mourning to get to our morning? As strong women, we want to declare that morning has come, hard times are gone and only joy remains.

What if Instead of jumping over and suppressing emotions (which never ends well for women), we learned the deep joy that comes from walking in step with the Father through the valley. Whether we are laughing or crying is not what matters. What matters is the developing of the deep truth that through every season of life, we possess the joy of the Lord. The joy of knowing that God is truly our strength and we don't have to worry about the mixture in our bottles. We don't have to be ashamed of them or hide them away. Instead we're free to pour them out at the feet of Jesus knowing that He is faithful to take care of our hearts.

Today I pray over you that whether it's the loss of a relationship, person, job or opportunity, that you would see Jesus in your mourning. I declare freedom from the pressure to suppress your emotions and release you into processing in-step with the Lord. I pray that the valley in your life would be in this moment filled with the light, love and presence of the Father. That you wouldn't attempt to hide away your disappointments, but instead use them as an avenue to the heart of God, and allow Him to eclipse them all with His joy. And I declare that in every place you have sown tears, that this would be the day that you would reap joy..

Today I pray that as you read, God would release the grace to let go. He knows where it's hard, He knows where it hurts. And He knows where He's taking you. I declare that you would receive the ability to discern between the call to move on and the call to persevere. And I pray that today as you listen, the Holy Spirit would visit you with His Peace as you face the changing seasons of your life, together.

"I will give you a new heart"

Day 10: The tenderizer

My husband and I have been married for about 5 ½ years. And in those years I'd say we have weathered quite a bit. Overwhelmingly the challenges that we have faced have been ones we've taken on side-by-side, but I remember very early in our marriage when we were still learning what it meant to battle things as a team.

I remember one night after we had a serious run in with each other. I don't say fight because there was no defense in the matter. He had hurt me, he knew it, and now here I was sitting alone on our couch prepping myself to get "tough". I would show him that I could be cold, that I could be sharp. I would make sure he knew how bad he hurt me ... sound familiar?

As I sat there justified in my living room thinking of all the ways I could emotionally hold out from him to make him "pay", the voice of the Lord spoke. He whispered to me through my tears, "If you will let me deal with your heart, I will heal you softer and more tender than you've ever been before".

Excuse me ... what? I mean was that even a thing? No Lord, I forgive my husband, but I think he needs to feel how wrong he was. I mean wasn't it my duty to hold him hostage by my actions so that he could see clearly how uncomfortable I could make life if he ever disappointed me again? Apparently not.

Ezekiel 36:26 says, "And I will give you a new heart, and a new spirit I will put within you. And I will remove the heart of stone from your flesh and give you a heart of flesh" ESV

If you're reading this and you're a woman I know you know exactly what I am talking about. As modern American women, we've been trained by our culture to be strong and resilient. We've been trained to be independent and to need no one. So, what happens when that culture clashes with an upside-down Kingdom? Where our world says, "what doesn't kill you makes you stronger", Our King invites us to yield our hearts and allow Him to be our defense in seasons of attack and hurt.

Of course, I am not saying we become weak or subservient. What I am saying is very much to opposite. The moment I decided to not harden my heart in my self-righteousness was the moment Holy Spirit was able to give me eyes to see my husband as His son, and allow me to partner with Him to love and encourage my husband in a way that I couldn't have in the natural. And there is nothing weak about that.

I understand that it's not an easy posture to take. I mean sometimes it is, but the closer the relationship, the higher the stakes, the harder it is sometimes to release the grace to someone that only we can. If you think about it, God has given you to the people in your life just as much as he's given them to you. He has given others a specific grace for our weaknesses and short comings, and he's given us people that need our grace in return.

Today I want to pray Ezekiel 36:26 over you. I pray that you would allow God to confront the stony, hardened, hurt places of your emotions, and in exchange, give you a soft and pliable heart. I speak over situations that have tried to leave a stain or battle scar on your heart, and I declare that there is no need to fight, because the Lord alone is your defense. God, I thank you for grace over every woman reading these words. I release the bravery to surrender emotions to You, and trust that You are good and are walking them through to perfect healing. I release over them a fresh baptism of joy that baffles the natural mind. And I thank you that today you lead them in paths of righteousness for Your name's sake. Thank you, Jesus for being so tender with our hearts. By Your strength we will choose to feel, we will choose to heal and we will choose You again and again.

> "Fear not, for you will not be ashamed"

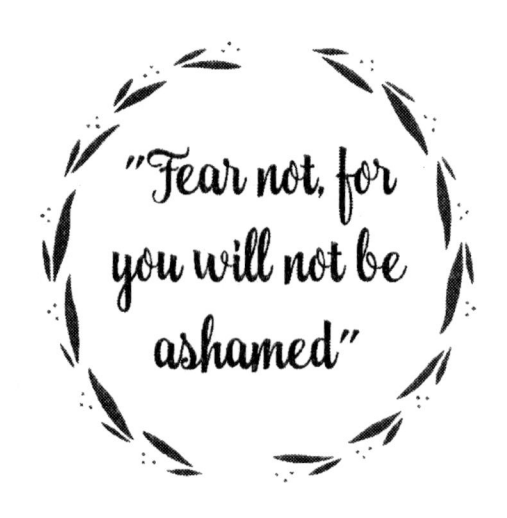

Day 11: Leading by living

Did you ever play "follow the leader" when you were in school? Have you ever looked around for the leader to follow and realized the leader, was you?

On my blog (NatalieEpps.com), there are times when I feel like everything I write says, Hey guys! I'm not totally healed yet, thanks for checking in. And if my readers get tired of reading it, imagine having to say it? It's like being single at Christmas... again. Everyone wants to know if you've met anyone nice, and all you can do is smile as big(ish) as you can at grandma or aunt so-and-so and say, "Not yet!"

This is where I live.

And yet I can't stop writing. Because in the process of this journey I have had some of the most intense God encounters of my life... and have met some of the most amazing people.

Take my speech therapist for example... She is a GEM! You know when you sit down to coffee with someone and ten minutes later you've already talked about your husband, kids and mom fears? And regardless of what their impression of you is you've already decided you're keeping them forever? Just imagine that minus the coffee (sometimes) plus her electrifying my face for 30-minute intervals, and that's our relationship! And so as much as I have days where I just can't understand why these things happened, I also can't imagine not having met some of these people, or some of the incredible life-giving conversations I've had. It's just hard to imagine life differently. And these past few weeks I feel like God has really started showing me just how valuable all these experiences have been.

One of the things that has continuously pulled me through my toughest times has been meeting/talking with someone who is on the other side of where I am. So many times, in life I've underestimated the power of leading by example and what it truly can do for those around us.

One Sunday at church I was worshipping and telling God, "I feel like you're giving me these opportunities to say yes. And I want to, I just wish I was a little further along in my healing." To which I felt God reply, "And that's exactly why I'm giving you opportunities... because you're not where you want to be, you're where I want you to be."

What? Dang

When you think about training in life, it always has a purpose it leads up to. Athletes train their bodies for a game or race, moms prepare to give birth, students study for a test. There is always an event to measure your preparedness.

In my mind, I always imagined there would be an "arriving on the other side" of this journey. I imagined I'd write a final blog post that said something to the effect of "well this is it folks, my last post. I've come through and I'm moving on". While I deeply believe that I'm continually "coming through" I find that there is less of a "moving on" and more of a change of scenery.

And where I keep waiting for that moment of "moving on", I'm realizing that maybe God is waiting for me to wake up to the fact that He has plans for me in the places where I don't feel prepared. It's like I've trained for a race, I've built up the endurance, I've eaten the right foods, I bought the right clothes, and I find myself at the starting line without any shoes... and God's saying, go ahead and run, we've got this.

What I learn more each day is that there is not a thing in our life that we will overcome or achieve that won't require faith. That sounds elementary but hear me out. I think sometimes we have this thought that we'll need faith as we prepare but once we're prepared we won't need it to step out. I want to propose to you today that, that is not faith. Faith is giving your "yes" when you want to say, "not yet".

One day as I was praying, God gave me this word. He was showing me how people have these huge "yes's" in their hearts. They want to say yes to the plans of their life, the great adventures and passions they feel on the inside of them. But how at the same time, the surrounding situations in their life are saying, "not yet".

God reminded me of Paul in prison. Paul could have assessed the situation and thought, ok, first things first, I need to get out of jail, get back to my people and then we'll regroup and get out and start sharing about Jesus again. But instead Paul decided to turn that prison cell into a worship services. Instead of saying "not yet" he said "yes" and started praising God with all his heart in a moment where he was stuck. And that was the moment God met him and literally broke the chains off his body that were holding him back.

God showed me how Paul could have waited for his situation to line up. He could have just waited until he was out of jail, regrouped and continued on with what God had called him to, but he would have completely missed the chance to build history with God in that moment. History that said, when I don't feel ready, when I feel stuck, my God shows up anyway. And through this journey I've learned that those are the moments that will change your life.

I believe it would have been really encouraging for Paul to see someone break out of their chains first. It would have added weight to his faith. But for him how much more incredible and personal was it that God showed up when he said "yes" and set Paul free? When I see someone overcome I'm encouraged... but when I overcome there's nothing that can stop me.

So, I come back around to my original statement. Sometimes the most inspiring, life-giving thing can be seeing someone else on the other side of where you are. But sometimes you go looking and you don't find it. And what I want to say to you today is that maybe you can't find it because God's asking you to be the "yes" in a sea of "not yets". There are so many more people that will come behind us... and when they come what will they find? They're looking for someone to give them hope that what's in their heart is possible, that they can get to the other side, but to do that... they need to see you, they need to see me. They need to see that someone else had the courage to whisper "yes" when their fears were screaming, "not yet". Will they find us leading by living?

So today my encouragement to you is to take your eyes off what's not yet done and put them on the One who's with you on the journey, and who is faithful to complete what is started. Do one thing today that you didn't do yesterday, and take a step towards your "yes"

> "Ask a sign for yourself from the Lord"

Day 12: Song birds

Have you ever had something happen where you felt like God was "winking" at you?

One of my most cherished possessions is a black bound journal that belonged to my dad. My dad had a gift for writing though he didn't use it much. I remember when I had an essay to write or a book report due, he would always be happy to read it for me. It never failed that when he handed it back over, the words on the page were the same, but something about how he had rearranged things would just make the words sing.

During his battle with cancer he told me one night that he had begun writing down his thoughts. In the aftermath of his passing, my brothers, Jonah and some others had gone to start sorting out his apartment. Of all the things I had experienced surrounding his death, for some reason that trip was something my heart just couldn't handle. I asked Jonah and my brothers to please look for his journal and bring it back to me. That evening they returned and handed me a small black book. I immediately headed upstairs and shut myself in a room. I wasn't sure who I would encounter in these pages. Was he mad? Was he sad? What I found as my tears dripped off my face onto the pages, was hope. He hadn't filled many pages, but the ones he did were full of stories of his encounters with a real and tangible God. These stories are so precious to me.

Each have taken on a life of their own and worked their way into my life's story. One in particular was an entry he wrote on a Sunday morning about a month before his death. He was processing with God as he laid in bed too sick from his last chemo treatment to make it to church. He was Laying out his thoughts and fears to God. As he was writing he said he asked the Lord for a sign that He was listening. He wrote about how song birds that began to sing outside of his window and how their simple, joyful song was all the sign he needed.
I remember a month after my wedding I woke up one morning in the upstairs bedroom of the condo my dad had found and sold to us. That morning upon waking I remember distinctly thinking, "I can't hear the birds". Their song had become a symbol to me in the mornings of the continual presence of God through the storm I was experiencing.

Lying in bed that morning Holy Spirit began speaking. He assured me that the birds song would always be a reminder to me of my dad and the goodness of God, but that He was ready to give me a new song and sign of His presence. It was a moment of knowing that I was being invited into the next step in my healing.

Isaiah 7:11 says, " Ask a sign of the Lord your[a] God; let it be deep as Sheol or high as heaven." ESV

I was never a big "sign" person. I wasn't against it, but it just never occurred to me to ask for something so physical ... obviously, a lot has changed. There are so many stories I could tell. I guess I could sum them up by saying that I am so thankful for the mysteries of

Heaven.

I know that as you're reading this there are things that are popping into your mind as special signs the Lord has given you at different times in life. Maybe those things started off constant and strong, but now are sporadic with weeks or months in between happenings.

Today I want to encourage you that you're not hearing God any less. Possibly it's that you're simply entering into a new place of progression with the Father. There are songs and signs for seasons that God gives to us, and as we change, so do they ... and it's OK. It's not always easy to heal, as crazy as that sounds. Healing brings a different kind of discomfort. But today I believe that if you'll take the chance with the Father and let Him lead, what you will find is that there are new songs and signs in this season to be seen and heard that are waiting to bring a new level of healing and experience into your life.

Today I want to pray over the song birds in your life. The special things that God has given to you as a sign of His presence with you. God, I ask that you would open the ears and eyes of your daughters to what you are trying to show them through the Earth. I pray encounters today over their life. That as they open themselves up to you that they would pick up on the song birds for their season. Intensify your signs in our midst God. Bring back to memory where you have reached through to us before, and allow us to see the open windows of Heaven and the good gifts you are giving to us through the world around us.

> "You are our potter; and all of us are the work of Your hand"

Day 13: Staying still when you want to run

Have you ever had a friend, spouse or leader who has told you something about you that you didn't particularly want to hear?

Oh, the joys of relationship.

Before my husband and I married we did the best thing we ever could have. We signed up for pre-marital counseling with the assistant pastor of our church and his wife. We would visit their home every other week and discuss different topics related to our upcoming nuptials. It was a very rewarding experience, and also at times a really hard one.

I'll never forget the hardest conversation we ever had. I was generally a sarcastic and quick-witted person ... still can be. I was hardly found without something to say, and in a recent event had taken my tongue too far and really hurt some of those close to me. I'll always remember the pastor looking me in the eye and after some silence and discomfort saying, "Natalie, people don't like to disagree with you because of how mean you can be." Now mind you I am sparing A LOT of context from this story. Basically, all you need to know was that I was at a place in my life where I didn't hear a lot of correction from others ... and it wasn't for lack of material.

I remember being so mad. How dare someone say something like that to me? Who were these people to call me mean? Thoughts began to stream through my head. I wanted so badly to spring off that couch and leave. I wanted to stand up and stop the conversation. I wanted my fiancé to jump in and defend me ... but he didn't. And as I sat there thinking of where I would go if I left, the reality of what my pastor was saying began to sink in, "I love you and Jonah too much to let you stay the way you are." His voice cracked as emotion filled his throat. "One day I'll give an account for the role I've had in your life." And as I closed my eyes and tried to ignore his words, it hit me like a ton of bricks ... he was right. I was completely unapproachable in correction, totally prideful and definitely on a path to destroy my marriage before it even began if I chose not to change.

Right there on their couch I broke into a million pieces. "You're right!" I cried. I was so sorry thinking of all the people in my life who were too intimidated to share the truth with me. Of course, our pastors were amazing and loved on me as I processed through what had just happened. And in the days after that meeting I went to each of the people I knew were impacted by my actions and I apologized. It wasn't because anyone told me to, or required it, but because I wanted them to know how much I valued them and needed their voices in my life.

Isaiah 64:8 says, " But now, O Lord, you are our Father;
we are the clay, and you are our potter; we are all the work of your hand." ESV

Sometimes the hardest thing to do is stay on the wheel. I wanted nothing more in that moment than to fly off that couch. No one talks about how good it feels to be corrected. No one raves about getting slapped back on the wheel to be molded again and again... but this is where our character is built. This is the place where the Lord sees just how willing we are to yield to his work in our lives. An artist knows what he wants the end product to look like, and generally only He can see the beauty in the mound of clay.

Today my prayer for you is that just like the moment I had, that you make the choice to yield to the voice of God in your life. And today instead of pushing away from the wheel to achieve momentary relief from the heat of God, that you throw your arms up and surrender to His gentle redirection. I pray for the tender mercies of God for you today, I exhort you in your bravery and I release grace over you for the hard places. Today I declare over you that as you brave the Potter's wheel, that you will find your heart becoming molded closer and closer to the image of who He is.

Today my prayer for you is that just like the moment I had, that you make the choice to yield to the voice of God in your life. And today instead of pushing away from the wheel to achieve momentary relief from the heat of God, that you throw our arms up and surrender to His gentle redirection. I pray for the tender mercies of God for you today, I exhort you in your bravery and I release grace over you for the hard places. And today I declare over you that as you brave the Potter's wheel, that you will find your heart becoming molded closer and closer to the image of who He is.

"The Father of mercies and God of all comfort, who comforts us"

Day 14: Responsibility to heal

Have you ever resisted healing?

If you've ever hung out with a toddler for long enough, one thing you'll learn is that there are a lot of things they need to tell you. These things range from what they ate that day, friends that are mean to them, where they put a random toy, something thing they can't find and of course my all-time favorite, where all their boo-boos are. My daughter looks at every freckle on her body as justification for the use of another glittery band-aid. I know you know what I'm talking about. It's like boo-boos are badges of honor, and every toddler is competing to be the most decorated.

We think it's funny... or annoying depending on how many we've seen that day. But one thing I've learned over the last several years is how as adults we strangely do the same thing. Maybe it's not our scraped knee or sparkly band-aid we want to show, but we certainly do have a knack for holding on to our hurts, and pointing them out to anyone who will listen.

2 Corinthians 1:3-4 says, "Blessed be the God and Father of our Lord Jesus Christ, the Father of mercies and God of all comfort, 4 who comforts us in all our affliction, so that we may be able to comfort those who are in any affliction, with the comfort with which we ourselves are comforted by God." ESV

Several weeks back I started thinking on this concept of our responsibility as Christians to heal. So often we find the church made up of hurt people, operating through a broken filter, who end up hurting people. Band-aids on parade. But the Word urges us to allow ourselves to heal for the sake of leading others the Healer.

I understand the fear that can come from healing. As I have gone through my journey I have realized moments where I have hesitated in saying that I am healed. For example, there is this drawer in our kitchen that is filled to the brim with medical supplies. Gauze and tape and ointments galore. All things that have been required as I've gone from one surgery to the next. You would think I would have already thrown all of it away as an act of declaration of my health. But that was actually hard. There was a tiny piece of me saying, but what if... It wasn't until recently that I gathered it up and put it away in our general first aid stash.

The truth is that as the body of Christ, it is our responsibility to decide to heal. Yes, I said decide. I truly believe that when we avoid wholeness and build programs that help Christians live better hurt lives, that we empower the chains of not only ourselves, but others. Paul exhorts us that we have been given the ministry of reconciliation. What I am proposing is that we must be reconciled within ourselves first. Now I'm not saying that there are not processes to what God does... heck I am a walking process. But when Christ said he came to "set at liberty those captive" He actually meant it. And how can we expect the world to come into an experience of healing and health with God, if we won't first?

Healing takes courage. Healing takes bravery, healing takes shutting the door on our "buts" and "what ifs". But the best news of all is that it was already accomplished by Jesus on the cross. There isn't anything we need to add to His payment. We only need to, like Peter, step out of the boat. Sometimes our hurt can be a refuge; a place to hide. But I also know that Jesus has entered in to all of our hurting places from eternity and today is asking us to trust in His ability to do in us, what was already done to Him, on the Cross. The question is, will we let Him?

Today I want to pray for those of you who know God is calling you into a deeper place of healing in Him. I want to lift up those of you who may be nervous about making a proclamation of healing because of the "what ifs" of life. God, today I ask for bravery over your daughters. I declare the fullness of healing in body, soul and spirit. I thank you that you are not a God who does things half way. And so today I release wholeness over nervous hearts, and the revelation of how connected their healing is to the wholeness of others. Today whisper Your promises to our hearts. Breathe on us again with Your 'yes' and 'amen'. Remind us of the perfect nature of the Father and of the completed work of the cross.

> *"For it is God who is at work in you"*

Day 15: Free to fail

Have you ever needed someone to give you permission to fail?

The story I want to share with you today is not actually one of my own, instead it belongs to my husband. But as I prayed this morning about what to write, this was the story rose up in my spirit.

Let me start by saying that my husband is an incredible musician. Of course, I am terribly biased, but I assure you, bias aside, he is legit. I've always loved listening to him play and sing to the Lord. It has always drawn such a sweet presence. A presence that I believe rises from this gentle place of humility he lives in.

I'll never forget one night after he came home from worship practice. He was the worship leader at the church we attended, and he was experiencing his own set of challenges in leading a group of incredibly talented people. It was late and I had sat down with him while he ate his dinner at the tiny all-purpose table in our condo. Worship had been hard for him lately. The pressure to "hit it" or "make something happen" had become too much for him to bear. He sat across from me with tears in his eyes and said, "I just wish I knew what they wanted from me". The deep desire he possessed to worship before God had been eclipsed by pleasing man instead. Now let me take a moment to say this was not the fault of one man. Instead it was the combination of what was going on inside my husband clashing against the internal state of someone else, and the result wasn't good.

Now if you've ever seen your husband emotional you know how I felt in that moment. I wanted to take ahold of this person and shake them. I wanted to say, "can't you see how hard he's trying?" ... something 9 times out of 10 a wife should not do. So, since violence was off the table, I took a deep breath and encouraged my husband the best I knew how, knowing that this was something the Lord alone would have to work in him.

Fast forward to months later as my husband was working to get out from under this weight of performance. We were at church and it had been another morning of trying to get something off the ground, and feeling the effects of not "delivering". Thankfully that day one of our pastors approached him. As the wife, I don't always get the privilege of all the juicy details of conversation (men). But simply put by my husband, our pastor said to him, "you have my permission to fail". He could see that Jonah was stuck trying to please instead of worship. And instead of giving him a formula to follow, or a comparison of someone he could emulate, he simply released the words my husband so badly needed to hear. That statement released my husband from the mental prison he had been trying to play his way out of, and gave him permission to go hard after God. Whether we all went to another place of Glory in worship, or it was a flop, being freed from the pressure of doing or being something was life to him in that season.

Philippians 2:13 says, " for it is God who works in you, both to will and to work for his good pleasure." ESV

Today I really feel like someone needs to hear, "you have permission to fail". There is such a pressure out there to do the thing, the best, the first time you do it. When really in everything we do we are to partner with God as He is working in us for His pleasure. God created us for His pleasure. And responding to that pleasure is the place where we truly release Heaven on Earth.

Should we love excellence? Of course! Should we give ourselves a break in pursuing it so we can learn how to fail with Grace? Yea, I think that's just as important.

God didn't deliver us into a mental hostage situation. He didn't create us to suffocate ourselves by constantly measuring ourselves against an imaginary standard. And my encouragement to you today, is that if you are finding yourself in this place there are two things you need to do. The first is define what is this standard you are being held to? Is it making something happen in worship? Is it preaching powerfully under the anointing? Is it having a perfectly clean home, without an item out of place? Or is it simply struggling to be seen as enough. Now I want you to follow that leash to who or what is holding it. Is it an actual person? Do you need to right now, out-loud, release yourself from their opinions? Is it fear of being rejected? Is it simply the anxiety of being seen as you truly are?

Today I want to declare over you that it is the Father who is working in you to both will and do according to His pleasure. And today I pray that you would receive the freedom to fail. I declare that even now you would be released from the pressure to do or be something, and instead, pick up the light and easy yoke of the Lord. I pray that you would find delight and joy in partnering with the Holy Spirit in everything you do. And today, I pray that you would start having fun! I pray that you would start having so much fun in walking with the Lord that you would be sure you were doing something wrong. God, I thank you for your daughters. And I thank you that their gifts and abilities all originate with you. And I thank you that today you would replace anxiety with excitement. Give them a glimpse of who you see them as from Eternity. And stir up their passions and the fire to pursue them with their whole heart today.

"You surround me with songs of victory"

Day 16: Songs for your season

Have you ever thought about what your life would be like if it were portrayed as a movie? Have you ever wondered what the soundtrack would be?

One of my absolute favorite things in life is music. To me I see notes and words as being very similar things. When arranged properly and inspired, they both can sing. Words, just like a music, when written well can move you to laughter or tears.

I have always believed that music is one of God's preferred avenues in speaking to us. And just like the soundtrack of a movie, I believe He releases songs for our seasons.

For example, I remember my dad's all-time favorite Christian jam was Newboys, "He Reigns" ... followed closely by U2's "Bloody Sunday. That was my dad.

It was the morning of his memorial service. I didn't need to be there until later in the day but I had decided that morning that I wanted to go to church. I was getting ready and rehearsing the events to be held later that afternoon, including the worship I had asked my husband, Jonah, to lead us in. One of the songs I had asked him to play was Chris Tomlin's, "Our God". It was a newish song at the time, and it was the first song we sang at church the morning after I found out about my dad's cancer. It had become an anthem of hope to me in that season.

I'm pretty sure that no one expected to see me that morning at church. I wasn't really sure I wanted to be there either. but I knew I wanted to be with people. I was in the middle of putting on my makeup, while listening to worship music, when I heard Steffany Gretzinger's voice ring out from the bedroom room, singing "Our God". I put both hands on the vanity and dropped my head as tears began to pour out onto the counter. The song I had declared after I found out about his diagnoses and the song we would sing later that day. I knew God was in this moment with His hands on my shoulders... I could feel Him hot upon me. I let the moment wash over me, and wiped my eyes for round two of mascara. I picked back up the brush, when no joke Josh Baldwin starts singing, "with all Gods people singing Hallelujah, Hallelujah, He Reigns." Now, I have been in church a long time. Maybe it was just the ones I went to, but never was singing a Newsboys song as part of a Sunday worship set a thing. I was a puddle... this moment was not a coincidence, God wanted my attention, He wanted me to stop. I stood there with hot tears once again running down my face. As I lingered in the moment, the Holy Spirit began to speak... He told me He was "releasing back songs to me that me and my dad had given to Him through this battle. God had won. Death had not". It wasn't the ending anyone wanted, but God would not be found weak in this moment.

Psalm 32:7 says, "You are a hiding place for me; you preserve me from trouble; you surround me with shouts of deliverance." ESV

I know they are just songs, but just like the songs that David poured out to God in times of praise and trial, those same songs are the ones that left Jesus lips on the Cross (Pslam 22; Matthew 27:46).

I believe that just like in scripture, God plants moments in our past and stands in our future waiting for us to run in to them. Breadcrumbs, songs, prophetic declarations on the path of our lives to remind us of who is holding this whole thing together.

Maybe this sounds crazy to you. But today I encourage you to take a moment to think on the songs of the seasons of your life. What did they mean to you then, how did God meet you in them, and what is the song for the season you are in now? Listen and wait as I guarantee you the Lord is singing over you in this moment, reminding you of where He has been in your past and showing you where He is standing in your present and future.

Today I want to pray over the season that you are in. Whether it's a season or joy, sorrow, decision or clarity, I release the song of the Lord over you now. I declare prophetic songs to break through Heaven and anchor you right where you are today. God, I thank you that your word promises that you will surround us in every season with "songs of deliverance" and we receive those now.

> "Let your words be few"

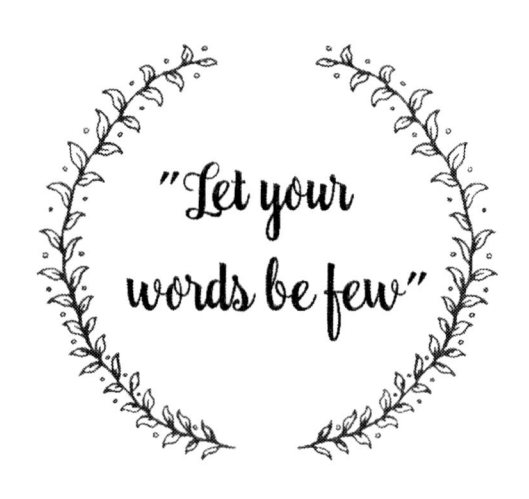

Day 17: Promises you shouldn't keep

Have you ever made promises you tried hard to keep? What about promises that you shouldn't have?

Years ago, I was walking through a hard time in one of my relationships. I had been hurt by someone I loved and though I was walking through it with friends and leaders, I was stumped at how the people in my life were treating this thing with so much grace and understanding. I had been hurt. I wanted justice! I wanted punishment and I wanted someone to come comfort me and validate all my feelings. And while people were certainly empathetic to my situation, the level of repercussion I wanted just wasn't happening.

I remember spending weeks asking God to bring healing to my heart. But it seemed that no matter how often I asked, the peace just wouldn't come. Then one evening in the middle of the night I was jolted awake. I was dreaming about this particular situation, and was determined to wake myself up. I stumbled out into my living room and sat down on the couch. I leaned my head back, closed my eyes, and asked God again to remove this pain from my heart.

As I sat there, the craziest thing happened. The Holy Spirit pulled back the curtain of my life and took me back to moments from years before where I had made statements out of my mouth that were now keeping me from the healing I was seeking. I had seen so many hurts conducted between my mom and dad's marriage and other broken relationships I had been a part of. And in an attempt to distance myself from the pain I was experiencing I remember how I had decisively rehearsed time and time again out of my mouth how "it" would never happen to me, how I would never deal with "it". Coming back to that moment on my couch, the Lord showed me the vows I had made, and how this rehearsing of protecting myself from pain had actually built a wall between myself and the healing and revelation God wanted to release. Yikes!

Ecclesiastes 5:2 says, "Be not rash with your mouth, nor let your heart be hasty to utter a word before God, for God is in heaven and you are on earth. Therefore let your words be few." ESV

Have you ever found yourself in this place? Have you ever experienced something or watched someone else experience pain? And in your heart, you built what you thought were boundaries of protection when it really turned out that you were building walls of defense?

I believe we have all faced these places in our life. We have seen an injustice happen and made declarations about what our portion will be. Now, I am not saying that is always wrong. We are to fill our words with truth and life, but I do believe there is a difference between speaking life and laying verbal bricks to keep out potential hurts. And we are the only ones who know the difference. But I believe that today the Lord wants to shine His light on those places. He is the discerner of our hearts, and knows when we are ready to receive His revelation. And it is the revelation He brings that leads not to momentary relief, but to lasting freedom.

Today I want to pray for revelation over you. I pray that God would shed His light on places where your words have kept you from breakthrough. I ask that by the grace of the Father you would be able to lower the walls in your life that have been built out of fear. God, I thank you for your daughters. And in this moment, I ask that you would release us from vows we have made out of fear or pain. I thank you that your goodness covers us and that your healing balm runs over the vulnerable untouched places of our heart. And today I declare a renewed sense of courage to face with the power of your Holy Spirit situations in our past that would pull lasting freedom into our present and future. No longer afraid, we trust your purposes in our lives and declare that with you we can face and traverse all things.

"You prepare a table before me"

Day 18: Your seat at the table

Can I tell you a secret? Jonah and I kinda have a thing with using disposable everything. I know it sounds terrible... but we seriously hate doing dishes. Our lives are currently on fast forward and by the time we finish our work for the day, get our girls home and make something that resembles dinner we have just a couple hours at best to spend together as a family before it's lights out for the girls as Jonah and I crash into the couch digging up any leftover energy we have for one another. So as un Earth friendly as it sounds, something had to go, and the dishes pulled the shortest straw. So if you come to our house and we pull out the real stuff, just know that means we're trying to impress you ;).

Anyway... now that my dirty secret is out... and now that anyone who has been to my home is trying to remember what they ate off of, I can move on to what prompted me to post today.

Let me ask you a question. Have you ever been to a dinner party?

I absolutely love having people over and trying new recipes. I've never been a cook. I always said when I got engaged I would learn. Obviously once I got engaged I was way too busy being in love to think about cooking... duh. So, when Jonah and I got married there was a lot of trial and error. Like I'm not kidding when I say boiling noodles was my arch nemesis ... it was bad. It was after I spent some time at home after my initial surgeries that hosting and cooking became some of my favorite things. I love preparing something for others to enjoy. I'm the person who dipped clementine's in egg wash and rolled them gold sugar glitter just to have something pretty to set on people's place setting at Thanksgiving... not that you asked for it, not that you're going to eat it, but you're welcome.

It's a sickness and there is no cure...

ANYWAY, glitter covered clementine's or not, when you're invited to a dinner party there is one thing you can be sure of. You may or may not know what's going to be served, you may not know who else is going to be there, but the one thing you can be certain of is that there will be a place for you. And the worst thing you can do when you show up is refusing to take your seat. Can you imagine you've been invited to a formal dinner and when you show up you insist on sliding up to the kids table instead? We would never want to insult a host by not appreciating their invitation... so why do we insist on doing it in real life?

Go with me for a second.

How many times have you had an idea or passion bubble up inside you? Maybe you want to start a company, start a garden or a family. Or how about starting a blog that you're convinced only your mom, siblings and husband are going to read? Just me? Doubtful. Listen to anyone talk long enough and their passions will tell on them. So why are there not more of us taking a swing at the things we love?

This past weekend I was thinking on receiving when out of the air it hit me. So many of us have convinced ourselves that we're somehow unqualified. Maybe we've convinced ourselves we don't have the time or money, or maybe that our dream plans are just that... a dream.

I was at church this past Sunday when this scripture popped in my head, Psalm 23:5 says, " You prepare a table before me in the presence of my enemies; you anoint my head with oil; my cup overflows." ESV

God has given us a seat at the dinner party of life... and we just need to take a seat.

God invited us (with help from our parents) into this thing called life. And He is letting us know through this verse that though there will be things and people that oppose us, He has prepared a place for us. A place where we can sit down in our rightful place in life and live to the fullest.

He didn't say, "Hey, I'm having a party if you want to come. But here's the thing, we're kinda short on space, so if you show up you're going to have to sit at the folding card table with the kids."

Now I know some of you just thought, "I'd prefer to sit with the kids". Any time you'd like to come over and sit with mine while I have dinner with my husband you just let me know ;).

The point is that before we can receive we have to realize that someone is giving. I know so many times in my life I've put off and delayed doing the things that make me happy out of fear of not being or having enough. The great thing in the Kingdom is that God set the table, cooked the meal and even rolled the clementine's in gold sugar glitter... all we have to do is show up and sit down. We've been invited and we're expected to show up.

So maybe it's time to RSVP. I know I want to show up in life. God says He has plans for me and that they are good. I want to know what they are and I want to see them come to pass. Maybe you don't believe in God. That's ok, because you were called to greatness far before you ever decided to believe or not. It actually doesn't take any permission on your part. It was done for you. Plans were put into play, and the Creator of the universe is inviting you in! Let's stop coming up with reasons why we can't and just jump in. Maybe your business won't be Fortune 500, maybe most of your garden will die and maybe you'll write a blog that only your mom, siblings and husband read ;).... but why not just go for it?

> "Honor instead of shame"

Day 19: Breaking shame

Do you ever feel like you're continuously apologizing for something in your life?

As you can imagine, when you are experiencing something like facial paralysis you tend to do what no person ever should ... and that is A LOT of googling. One thing I learned through my searching of Dr. Google, is that facial paralysis for the surgery I underwent is actually quite rare. Of 100 people operated on, approximately 3% will experience paralysis ... 3%! Now here I am, a "woman of faith" with literally all the odds in my favor, and I come out unable to move my face, blink, swallow or talk above a whisper. Not only did I feel like a failure to my Christian faith. I felt full of shame. I knew I did nothing to bring on this tumor, but still, I felt somehow responsible.

While "please" and "thank you" were ingrained into my vocabulary as a young girl, one phrase that I started using constantly after my surgery was, "I'm sorry". I don't mean as in I didn't learn how to apologize until then, but rather I found myself constantly apologizing to those around me. "I'm sorry for ruining plans", "I'm sorry you have to take care of the kids again.", "I'm sorry I look this way". I was constantly saying, "I'm sorry". And Jonah would always ask, "what are you saying sorry for?". The truth was that I didn't really know. I was just sorry for being me.

A few months ago, I was listening to a message by Kris Vallotton. As part of his message he was referencing a TED talk hosted by Berne Brown on "The Power of Vulnerability". During her talk she spoke about human connection, vulnerability and shame. And how shame holds the power to unravel human connection. In expounding on this thought, Kris Vallotton said something that completely un did me. He said, "conviction says we've done something wrong. But shame says I AM something wrong".

Right there in that moment my heart broke into a million little pieces. This was it. This was why I couldn't stop apologizing. I was living under the belief that somehow through this surgery, I had become something wrong.

Somewhere in me I believed that between saying goodbye to my husband in pre-op, and waking up with a tube down my throat, that I had climbed off the operating table and knowingly sabotaged my life and the lives of all those around me. And I had spent day after day crying a thousand tears because I felt like I had single handedly let everyone in my life down.

Thankfully, Isaiah 61:7 says, "Instead of your shame there shall be a double portion; instead of dishonor they shall rejoice in their lot; therefore in their land they shall possess a double portion; they shall have everlasting joy." ESV

Honor was the last thing I felt. Shame had become a name tag. I wore it for so long that it began to define me. The deceptive part was that it felt so right. I started to live from this place of, "This happened, so clearly and understandably it is hard for others to incorporate me into their lives. I'm just too much of an inconvenience"

But we know the truth.

Jesus became shame. And when I knowingly operate out of this place of shame, I am saying to Jesus that his trip to the cross was not enough. That not only must I "bear my cross" but I must also get up on it and pay for what He couldn't cover.

God desires for our shame to be replaced not just with honor, but He promises that a "double portion" will be ours. He desires and has declared over us that in exchange, "everlasting joy" will be given. The word says that Jesus "made a spectacle of sin and death". In His rising, He literally exposed and paraded the weakness of the enemy and his effect on our eternity. The actual truth is that though we may be walking something out today in our body (whether physically or emotionally), Jesus has already bore it from eternity. And today we have the authority to deny shame entrance into our hearts.

Today I want to pray honor over you. Maybe you're finding yourself in this story. Maybe you were the passenger to something that happened to you, and maybe you caused something to happen that has brought you to this place. Either way, today I declare that the honor of the Lord is upon you.

God, I thank you that when you see your daughter, you see Jesus. You don't see the stain of sin or life. You see the radiating face of your Son. Holy Spirit I release You in this moment to remove the weight of shame off of every person reading these words. I thank you that this shame has already been carried from eternity, and that today we are free to receive the "everlasting joy" You said belonged to us. And today I thank you that even memories of moments that carry shame would be cleansed by You. Lord you desire nothing but the fullness of Jesus in our lives. And today we say that we will make the exchange; our shame for your honor and joy.

"For we are His workmanship"

Day 20: Imposter

Have you ever felt like a fake?

In 2013 I had the "ah-ha" moment of my life. I remember a prophet came to our church for a weekend of services. He had called me forward and prayed for me during one of the meetings. Part of the word he kept coming back to and emphasizing was that He felt the Lord declaring over me that it was time to "lean in". I thought in the moment I knew what he was saying, but It wasn't until months later that the word came further to life.

I was big and pregnant with our first daughter, and found myself sitting one day in my baby's future nursery incredibly overwhelmed. I was trying to figure out my fairly new marriage, trying to cope with my ever-changing body and excelling rapidly in a surprising way working for a major financial institution as a "Corporate American" woman. As I sat gliding back and forth in my baby rocker I began scanning the tall bookshelf in her room. I wasn't particularly looking for anything as much as I was sorting out my thoughts from the day. It was as my eyes gazed over the rows of authors that a book suddenly jumped out at me. A white spine with red bold lettering yelling at me, "Lean In". The word I had been given months before came rushing back.

I immediately grabbed the book from the shelf and began to flip intently through the pages. It was a book written by a highly successful business woman, Cheryl Sandburg, and given to me by a fellow working mama. It was all about finding your way as you juggled multiple roles. Christian? No. Inspiring? Incredibly. It was after about a week of reading it that I stumbled across a gem that changed my life.

In the book, the author writes about a speech she heard as a young woman in college. It was a seminar entitled the "imposter syndrome". The focus of this talk was around the idea that no matter what women did in life, they weren't actually deserving of it. It's this idea that every relationship, promotion, gift and good thing they experienced in life was a fluke. And because they weren't actually deserving of any of it, at any moment all of these things could be taken away from them. What they actually were was an imposter ready to be found out.

My mouth about hit the floor... this was me. No matter how much I achieved as a new wife, or mom, or in my career, I couldn't shake the feeling that somehow it was in vain because what I truly was, was an imposter on the edge of being exposed. I wasn't a good wife or mom or career woman. I couldn't actually do any of it well.

And let's face it, we all have found ourselves in this situation at one point or another. Others admire what we do or who we are, but we can't accept the compliments because we don't feel worthy. The Bible, thankfully, is incredibly clear on this point.

Ephesians 2:10 says," For we are his workmanship, created in Christ Jesus for good works, which God prepared beforehand, that we should walk in them." ESV

The actual truth is that we are not fakes or imposters. We are daughters of the King who have been set up to receive the best that life can give. And I feel that in this season it is time to own that truth. It's time to stop being paralyzed by this lie and realize that it's the enemy who creates counterfeits, not our God. He has created paths of success in our lives. And if there is anything about our lives to be "found out" it's that there's so much more to us than we've yet discovered... and the world needs it.

So today I pray that this lie would be exposed in your life.
That right now in this moment with the Lord, He would pull back the curtain and show you where you've reduced yourself to a fake, when God sees you as legitimate. I pray that God would release revelation over you today to begin to bring situations, relationships and conversations into the perspective of Heaven. I pray that you would see that you are not an imposter, but rather the very image of God. And that as a daughter of the King, you are positioned and anointed to call out the counterfeit of the enemy, and restore others to their rightful, God-breathed identity.

"Let us go to the other side"

Day 21: In-between

Are you the type of person who gets so impatient after reading the first chapter of a book that you jump to the end?

As someone who has walked and is walking through a process with the Lord in my body, one very important thing I have learned through the journey is how vital it is to remember the moments "in-between".

I recently sat down to reflect on my journey over the last few years concerning my health. I pulled up my blog and began to read over the posts (you can find them all at NatalieEpps.com). In the early days after my first and second surgery I became desperate to see signs of improvement in my body. I woke up slowly each day. I would peel the tape off of my eyelid, which was left there the night before to keep it closed. I would pump myself up and convince myself that I could give it another day, I could get out of this bed. It was a routine that went on for weeks and months.

One day standing in my kitchen I had become emotional like I had so many days before. "God" I cried, "I don't know what to do with myself. I can't make anything happen. What do you want from me?" "Write", was the simple and immediate reply of the Lord ... so I dried my eye (only one currently tears), and began to scribble down the emotions that were pouring out of my soul.

Originally my blog began as an easy way for me to update family and friends on doctor's visits, second, third and even fourth surgeries. But as I continued to write it became a place where I could process externally what the Lord was doing in me both on the inside as well as the outside. What I found that day as I reflected back over my posts was that this had become the story of two very different people. Both hopeful, both with faith in God, both me... but very different.

It reminded me of the story from the Gospels where Jesus tells the Disciples to get in the boat and "cross over to the other side". The story starts with them boarding their fishing boat and ends with them arriving on the opposite shore, but what a robbery it would have been if the moments in-between had never been recorded.

The storm that rose up around them and threatened their very lives, and Jesus' intervention in quieting the waves were the very moments that changed who those men were from shore to shore. Maybe not the disciple's proudest moments, but it was the time in-between which developed confidence in them and enabled them to stand with new revelation along-side of Jesus, the storm silencer.

I believe that as you read this today that you have hopes of how you would react to the heat and pressure of life. Maybe like me, you've already been exposed to situations which have given you that opportunity. What I can say from experience, is that having an "idea" or "hope" of your response is good, but it's the moments that you learn in-between the shores of the seasons of your life that forge your response in challenge and opposition.

I love hearing testimonies of people who have arrived on the shore of their promise. Nothing spurs my faith more. But what I want to know more than how they acted when the "thing" came, is how they acted while they waited. And I venture to say that you do too.

What I want to pray over you today is that you would not discard the process. That you would not dismiss or become ashamed of the moments "in-between". I believe today that as you read these words that God is working between shores and deepening the anchor of your soul. Today I declare over you that you have not come behind. But that you are digging a well with God that will stand forever as a testimony of your life and of God's goodness. And that as your testimony leaves your lips that it would be the thing to encourage and spur others through the seasons of their life. We all have a story. And today I encourage you to be proud.

> "Because of my integrity You set me in Your presence forever"

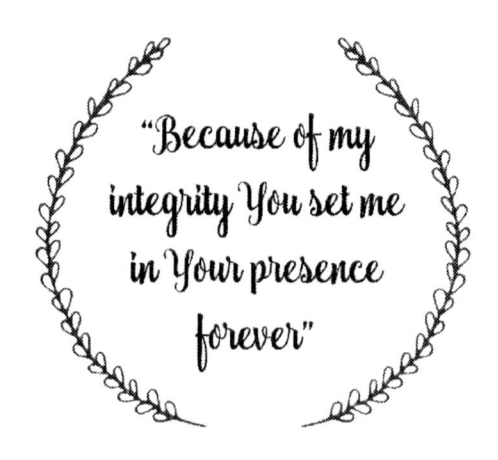

Day 22: Honoring your why

Have you ever tried to do something because someone else said you should? Or have you laid the guilt on yourself for not listening to someone else tell you why they wouldn't do what you're doing? I'm going to venture to say that if you're living and breathing, then yes you have.

I remember when my now husband and I were courting. Yes, I said courting. We had access to some of the best friends and leaders a person in a new relationship could hope to have. But you know how it is when you are in L.O.V.E. The sun and moon and stars all revolve around each other ... and we had it BAD.

Now our hearts were in the right place. We wanted a relationship that glorified God. We listened to counsel and set up rules and had accountability. But at the end of the day we "tried" so hard to do things the "right" way as prescribed by other people, that we failed good. And by good, I mean it was pretty bad.

Thankfully after all our pitfalls we still made it through a really purposeful courting and engagement relationship. God did a number on both of our hearts in ways that we are still benefiting from today.

The point of the story is that no matter what other people told us to do and no matter how right their advice was, it wasn't in our hearts. Our hearts were to do the right thing, but our motivation was to do the things we were told so we could be approved of ... and that my sisters is slippery slope.

Psalm 41:12 says, "But you have upheld me because of my integrity, and set me in your presence forever" ESV

Our intentions are to live with honor before the Father, but how many times have we done this? We hear a good story or message, we read a good article, and we set out to make a change or do something the right way. And how many times have we found ourselves failing miserably, because while the thing may have been noble and good, the motivation of our hearts were not in the right place.

I want to propose to you today, that in everything we do, we have to know our "why".

Jesus knew why He did everything He did. Every healing, every teaching, every time He broke with cultural norms, it came out of a deep place of understanding His "why". And spoiler alert, in case you haven't made it to the end of the story, His why was us.

Maybe today your thing isn't relationships. Maybe it's a performance mentality that creeps in where you constantly have that voice in the back of your head saying, "what would so and so think". Today I want to say that no matter what your vice is, your "why" must be rooted in the Father. People, positions and circumstances will come and go, but at the end of the day it will be you and Jesus. And He won't be asking why you didn't live like someone else.

I often think back on our situation and wonder how things would have gone if I had deeper convictions of my own. We all know there is no point on dwelling on yesterday, but today I encourage you to ask yourself, "Why do I do or not do things? What are my motivations?" Where have I found myself with the best of intentions, trying to achieve someone else's goals instead of my own?

Today I pray that your "why" would spring up and over take you. I declare freedom from the pressure to do something or be someone at the prescription of others. I ask that in this moment, God would begin to show you how deeply important you are, and how your why has the power to change the world around you. And right now, I release over you the freedom to wear it proudly. I break off timidity or any reservation in your heart that would speak up and try deter you from boldly being who you are before the Father today!

"From glory to glory"

Day 23: Lateral Moves

Have you ever felt like you were going from "hell to hell", instead of "high to high"?

When I'm not wife-ing or mom-ing, I am working. Being a "corporate American woman" definitely wasn't ever something on my radar. But like all things that are meant to be, when they click, they click!

Several months back I was asked to speak at an "Own Your Career" event at my work. These events feature people who have recently been promoted within the company. Guests join a panel of other employees and share their success stories, followed by a Q&A session. For this particular event, the moderator had sent out questions ahead of time. There were all the questions you might expect. The "who", "what" and "how" of our career progression, but the one question that stuck out to me above the others was, "Tell me about a time you made a lateral move and why".

Now for those who do not know, a lateral move in the corporate world is when someone takes a new job doing potentially more work for the same amount of money. Career progression is one of the main reasons people do this. They may not feel ready for a jump in position or paygrade, so they move laterally instead to gain experience. While I personally have never made an official "lateral move", it triggered in my mind one of the underlying themes that I have found to be true over and over again in my life. And that is the fact that I have never received a promotion in anything whether in work or life without first doing the work where I was planted.

Don't hear what I am not saying. I am not talking about works over grace. What I'm talking about is having eyes to see when something needs to be done and just doing it instead of waiting for someone to give you a badge or a title.

I remember I had just returned to work from maternity leave. I had met with my boss and he asked if I would be willing to help the department. There was a major project coming that would require longer hours, managing people, answering to executives, maintaining reports and stats. There was no title or promotion to go along with it, but it was work that needed to be done. Without hesitating I agreed. The project lasted longer than expected and was everything that my boss had said and more. And at the end of the day, as promised, there was no pay increase or title change. Instead, there was a pile of new experiences I now possessed.

Now don't get me wrong, I am not a money martyr. I literally have zero desire to work for free. My point is that I had my mind set on an eventual goal and while I wasn't ready to operate officially in that capacity, I was willing to use any experience to help get me there. And it was that experience that led to a promotion in the months following.

It makes me think of someone like Joseph. Talk about lateral moves. How about serious demotions? He had a call from the Lord as a young child to rule an entire Nation. And almost immediately after the release of that word he was faced with decades of rejection and oppression. But regardless of circumstance, in every situation Joseph found a way to be the best at what he was doing. If it was a palace servant or a prisoner locked in a cell, he found a way to become excellent wherever he was. He never waited for promotion to find him, instead he continually prepared for it.

2 Corinthians 3:18 says, "And we all, with unveiled face, beholding the glory of the Lord, are being transformed into the same image from one degree of glory to another. For this comes from the Lord who is the Spirit." ESV

The Word says that we are continually moving from Glory to Glory. It's no secret that in today's world we like everything instant. We love immediate gratification. But it leads me to think about the processes that we walk through with the Lord. While He is continually moving us from Glory to Glory, it can often feel like we're moving side-to-side instead of high-to-high. But today I want to share with you that I believe those moments of side-to-side are exactly what enable us to receive promotion from the Lord and leave one place of His Glory for another.

So today I want to pray patience in the process over you. I pray and encourage you to dig into the place you currently are, instead of looking off into the distance. I declare that any residue of comparison would fall off of you now. I declare that like a runner running, you wouldn't focus on looking side-to-side, but that you would focus in this moment on the path the Lord has laid out for you. And I pray that today God would take you higher to see your progress, and plunge you deeper into His assurance and He positions you for the next place of Glory.

"I am the vine; you are the branches"

Day 24: Growing Weeds

Have you ever thought you were making the right choice, only to find out that you were dead wrong?

Let me start today by saying that I am NOT a gardener. I was born with two thumbs and, unlike my mother, neither of them are green. I need things like succulents in my life. Succulents basically thrive on being starved just shy of death … those are my kind of plants. Any other plant killers out there?

Anyhow, this past Spring I was so encouraged at the signs of life after another gray Ohio winter that I became inspired. This was the year that I was going to grow something! I can only imagine what my poor husband thought. He has a front row seat to all my antics. At this point in our relationship I think he's realized that even when he sees disaster ahead, sometimes it's best to just step aside and let me do "my thing".

So anyhow, with dreams of Eden in my head, I jumped in my car and headed to the hardware store. It was around Mother's Day and my little sister had just bought me some Cilantro and Basil, so I added a couple of strawberry plants and a lavender bush, and BAM, I had a little back deck garden. Now the healthier my little plants looked, the more ambitious I got. One day looking at my plants I thought, I am going to grow tomatoes.

To be honest, I don't even love tomatoes. But something about growing them sounded fun. Now I didn't want a normal already grown tomato plant. Oh no, I was a professional, I was going to grow them from seeds. One pot, a little bit of soil and some Pinterest surfing and before I knew it I had a tomato plant harvest in the making.

And then, I waited. And I waited, and waited, and waited. I wanted to grow something SO bad, and one day on my way out the door as I stopped to take inventory of my little garden, I spotted them, little SPROUTS! I was so proud of myself. Now as days went by more and more sprouts appeared. A few looked different than the others, but like I said, I am not a gardener so I just kept watering and sunning them.

One Friday morning I remember I was up early meeting with a group of ladies I pray with weekly. One of the ladies was praying about new growth and things springing forth. Naturally my mind wandered to my little garden. I started thinking about those tomato plants and how I notice that they didn't all quite look the same. I know it's really spiritual of me, but I got distracted and suddenly a thought hit me ... "oh my gosh, I am growing weeds!"

After the call ended I jumped off the phone and ran outside. I downloaded a plant app and took some pictures. And in just a few short moments technology told me what I couldn't figure out on my own ... I in fact was growing a pot of weeds. And not just growing them, I was cultivating them. I loved those weeds! So embarrassing.

A little while later while driving to work I was thinking on my morning weed revelation. I started to think about in the word where it talks about the wheat and the tares. They grew together for just enough time, so that by the time the tares were detected they ended up threatening the life of the entire crop. I also thought of the parable about the seed and the soil. Some of the seeds fell into the ground and began to grow, but thorns began to grow up with them. And again, because they were not detected, they ended up choking out the good seed. Maybe it's a far jump to make, but it seriously got me thinking … where else in my life was I protecting things that I saw as good when really the Lord was trying to up root them?

Sometimes it's hard to tell the difference when our hearts are involved. Maybe it's a job or relationship or opportunity. You want it to happen so bad that you don't notice the tares. I know in my life there have been times where I have wanted to hear a "Yes" so badly that I've blazed past the neon, blinking, "No" sign in my front yard. It happens to me, it can happen to you, it happens to the best of us.

Today I want to pray for the gift of discernment over you. God, I ask that in this moment you would reveal to us our hearts and places where we have protected tares that you are trying to root out. I pray that you would give us the ability to see correctly choices or people or moves in our life that may be a detour from your plans. And I ask for your gentle course correction. Today I declare over each woman reading this that you would be encouraged that the master Gardener is in your midst. And that revelation would spring up in your life shedding light on the plans of the Father for you in this season.

"And you will be given a new name"

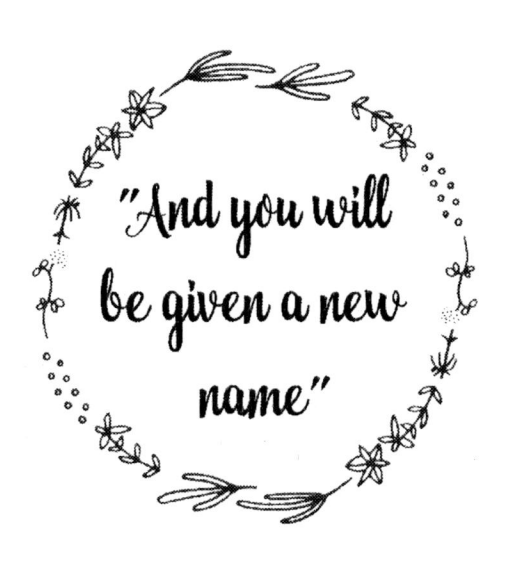

25: A New Name

When I was preparing to marry Jonah all I could think about was being his wife. I would sit and imagine the life we would lead together. The places we'd go, the children we'd have... basically I had no idea what I was actually getting into. I mean believe me, we had some amazing premarital counseling. Nothing was wrong with our relationship, we just believed in going into marriage with as much support as possible, instead of waiting until something went wrong. But alas, even with the best advice in the world it was still impossible to know just what was waiting for us around the corner. And in my fairy tale state I couldn't see anything making me happier than becoming "Natalie Epps".

Our wedding was amazing, in my humble opinion. And the honeymoon was awesome. We couldn't have hoped for anything better. After a time away we returned to our new home and as much as we wanted to live in our happy little cloud, it was back to life as usual and all that came with it.

I remember the day I went to the license bureau to change my name. Previously I had been so eager to become an "Epps". But standing in line at the BMV that day I felt my heart sink a little. My dad had just passed away and I felt myself in that moment wanting to hold on to my old name. To me it was like keeping my name would somehow keep him alive a little longer. "Couldn't I just be married to Jonah and keep my dad's name?", my mind started to race. Now, this is not me telling anyone what to do about taking names. I just know for me in that moment that God calmed my heart as if to say, "it's ok, take his name". And so, I did.

Fast forward to several months ago in church. During worship two of the leaders were taking about how God wanted to give new names. If you don't know anything about the Bible there are several stories where God changed the name of a person, and when He did their lives were altered drastically. As they spoke I could feel my heart begin to beat faster so I leaned in. I felt the Lord challenge me saying, "I want to give you a new name, but you're still waiting for the old one to be restored"... and He wasn't talking about my maiden name. For the longest time walking through my journey of healing I had found myself thinking, "if I could just be restored to who I was, then I would be ready for something new". In that moment, I knew that God was asking me to lay down waiting on something old to be restored and grab ahold of the new thing He was doing.

Isaiah 62:2 says, "The nations shall see your righteousness, and all the kings your glory, and you shall be called by a new name that the mouth of the Lord will give." ESV

New can be scary, and I know you can relate. Insert yourself into that moment if you haven't already. You are comfortable with the "old" you. You know what that bar looks like. But let go? What does that look like? In that moment for me, I was suddenly so aware that God wanted to do something new in me, but He couldn't get me to let go of who I used to be. The old was familiar, the new was uncertain... I knew I still had the choice to say no, but I didn't want to.

And I know that many of you reading this today can relate. You feel the Lord wanting to give you a new name, but for some reason you're afraid. And today I believe that God is asking you to lay down the bar of who you used to be, and pick up the possibility of what the future could hold. The Lord is a gentleman, He's not going to force you to do anything... He literally can't. But He can create the opportunity for you to choose to let go and grab on to Him. Grab on to a new name. And today I believe that your heart has been prepared for this place.

Today I pray courage over you. Courage to let go of who you used to be. I break off any thought in your mind that whispers to you that you were better "when". God, I thank you that in this moment you are replacing the labels of who we thought we were or who people told us we were, with your seal of sonship. Today I declare that we are stepping out into the new waters of who you are calling us to be. Thank you for wiping away disappointments and breathing fresh on us in this moment. We welcome the new name of the Lord, and we say that with you we are not afraid of what the future holds. We trust you and we believe that with you working in our lives that the result will be good.

> "Give thanks in all things"

Day 26: Staying Thankful

Have you ever found yourself struggling to stay thankful?

On April 7th Jonah and I celebrated five years together. As we have each year since being married, we sat down to a nice dinner and took stock over the last few years. I believe it's so important to take time as a couple to remember and specifically call out the times and areas where God has shown Himself faithful. As we sat that night talking about the challenges we had encountered, my face that was finally showing signs of life and the beautiful girls we were raising, I was suddenly overwhelmed with emotion. No, facial weakness, five hospital stays and four surgeries never once sounded like "fun". A brain tumor and a parent dying prematurely never entered my mind as part of the "plan", but as we sat talking I took a deep breath as a word given to me in the year previous washed over me. "You will not be disappointed". It was true that times had been trying. The things we had faced in a short amount of time were enough to age anyone. But instead in a moment where I could have been disappointed, I was thankful.

I know it can be human nature to focus on the things that are not going well in our lives, instead of celebrating the areas that are flourishing. We have all been guilty of this at one time or another. But that night as we talked, we recounted how the year as my first surgery was also the same year that we welcomed our youngest daughter into our family. Somehow, in all of the muck of just struggling at times to make it to the next sunset, we had almost skipped over one of the most joyful moments of our marriage. We have an incredible three-year-old and sweetheart of a two-year-old. We have wonderful family, incredible friends. We don't have it all together or right, but we have the Lord and we have each other.

1 Thessalonians 5:18 says, "give thanks in all circumstances; for this is the will of God in Christ Jesus for you." ESV

I want to talk for a moment today about this verse. The temptation I have found in my own life, is that once hardship or tragedy is experienced, human nature tends to subtly reinterpret the scripture. And it happens when the "this" in verse 18 gets replaced with "what" I am going through. When I do that what I am saying is, "give thanks because this (sickness, tragedy) is Gods will for me." And while that may help me find a temporary resting place for the questions of the heart, it is a terrible misrepresentation of scripture. It sounds nice, but really, it's just an "out" for the areas of our life that we can't classify. And you don't have to have experienced something exceptionally terrible for this to happen. I find we do it with others too. We want so badly to have an answer, that sometimes we give a lame one. I know I am guilty.

The harder thing sometimes to say, and what God actually desires for us, is that we would live a life full of thankfulness. Sickness and tragedy are never His will. And when we abandon the "easy" answer and instead press in to life from a posture of continual thankfulness, we then are able to grab a hold of hope when it seems its light is at its dimmest.

I heard it once said that, "you make choices and eventually they make you". It's so true. We make choices to be negative or positive every day. Eventually the pressure of life comes, and when it does, what we've chosen to put in is what makes its way out.

Thankfully the Bible says about Jesus that, "we have this hope, an anchor to our soul, firm and secure." I'm a visual person, so I look at it like this. There's a boat in the water. A storm comes and the boat rolls with the wind and clashes against the waves. But what the storm doesn't know is that far beneath the water, the boat's anchor is firmly planted.

Right now, you may be in the midst of a storm. From an aerial view, it may look like you are being thrashed and rocked by the waves. It may look like you are done. But today I want to encourage you to take ahold of hope once more. The surface of your life might be raging, but beneath the surface Jesus is your anchor, firm and secure. You may feel that you are drifting from the site of the anchor, but I assure you that the anchor will always pull you back.

God, I pray over each (person/daughter) reading these words today. I pray that their hearts would be full of thankfulness towards you. I ask that you would show yourself to us in the hard places, and that you would reveal yourself to us today as our anchor. I declare that today you would infuse us with hope. That the lame situations that come at us in life would find no resting place. And that as we live from a posture of thankfulness that every bearer of depression and cynicism would find themselves in better moods just by being around us. And Lord if we are those people, we simply ask for more of You. Thank you for being our anchor and rock. Thank you for being an immovable fixture of goodness in our lives. And I ask today that as we go, that you would douse us in your peace and love

> *"I know the plans I have for you says the Lord"*

Day 27: Timeless

Have you ever had something happen in your life that you weren't expecting? Have you ever wondered "where was God?"

After my dad died I remember a very dear friend of mine talking to me about my upcoming wedding. He had passed away almost exactly a month prior. She was doing her best to encourage me and in doing so said, "your wedding is still going to be perfect." I remember my heart being stung by those words. How on earth could my wedding be perfect? That was a literal impossibility. I knew it would be beautiful, I knew it would go smooth and I knew I would be marrying the love of my life… But perfect? No.

I did my best to smile and say, "I know", but inside I couldn't disagree more. There had been so little time to think about anything that it hadn't even crossed my mind how "not perfect" I was convinced things would be. In the days following I found myself sitting, looking out a window asking God how she could say something like that knowing it couldn't be true. As I sat with the Lord, He spoke and said, "you didn't know this would happen, but I did. I've already stood at your end and have seen your wedding. And from the perspective of Heaven, it is going to be perfect." I felt like the wind had been knocked out of me. My heart couldn't immediately catch up, but I knew in that moment that He was right, and so was my friend. From Heaven, the Father was letting me know that He had already seen not only my dad's passing, but also my wedding day. He had already been present in both.

Jeremiah 29:11 says, "For I know the plans I have for you, declares the Lord, plans for welfare[a] and not for evil, to give you a future and a hope." ESV

In life, there are so many things that we never see coming, both good and bad. And some things cannot be avoided, but rather must be walked through. But in every season of our lives one thing is true, and that is that God always makes a path leading straight to Him. He's already stood at your end, just as He is standing now in your present, and He's working it together for your good.

We stand in this thing called time. And God is timeless. He has the ability to stand in our past, present and future all at once. And while the temptation exists to say, "if you were there then why wouldn't you stop this thing from happening", the greater comfort is knowing that when we are blind-sided by our present, we serve a God who holds our future. And has already declared that it is good.

Today I want to pray for those of you looking back at a time and wondering where the Father was. Or maybe you know He was there, but the sting is still very real. God, I thank you for your sweet daughters. I thank you that you alone hold every one of our days, and you know that they are good. God, today I declare that Your peace would fill our hearts. As painful memories come I thank you that the revelation of your ever-present love would overtake us and remind us that that not one of our moments is lost in You. And God I ask that in this moment You would reveal to us the fullness of your goodness and prosperous plans you have for our future.

> "Behold, I am doing a new thing"

Day 28: Coats in the Summer

We all have these friends ... maybe you are this friend. You know who I'm talking about. The one who the day after Christmas will post a meme on social media from "ELF" stating, "Only 364 days till Christmas" ... yea that friend. I see you!

Now don't get me wrong. I am an excitable person. I always love the next great reason to invite way too many people over to my house to have fun being together. In fact, I am three days out from my youngest daughter's second birthday party and I am PUMPED! But nothing, and I mean nothing, makes me more disgruntled than when stores rush seasons. It drives me crazy to see stores putting out their fall lines the weekend after the Fourth of July. Like, please, I live in Ohio, I don't get summers. Let me live in my denial and hold on to the little sunshine and warm weather for a little longer before you start displaying your sweaters and boots ...

Anyway... Back to my point.

I was spending time several months ago at a worship night with a friend of mine who embodies this person. It was August and she was telling me and few others about how she had opened her window that day and lit a Fall candle. Now before you take your flip flop off and throw it at her, listen to what she had to say.

She told us how Holy Spirit began speaking to her about how we prepare for seasons. She, like many of us, was in a season of transition and looking to the Lord for what was next. He began comparing how we prepare in the natural verses how we prepare in the spirit. In the natural, if we walk into a store in the middle of the summer and see a coat on sale half of us will think, "This is a great deal. I'll be so warm next winter". The other half will say, "That's crazy. Even if it's cheap, it's 90 degrees outside. I am not buying a coat".

In the same way, we can see a season change coming in the spirit. And in that moment, we have a similar choice to make. We can either know that we're not in that season yet, but see the benefit in starting to prepare, or we can look at it and say, "It's too soon".

I believe there are so many women in this place right now. I truly believe God has been releasing and breathing dreams and visions on so many, and even though the "thing" hasn't come to pass, He's inviting people to start physically preparing. Maybe there's a class He wants you to start taking, a business He wants you to look into, a trade to start learning about. This may not be the season of your voyage, but it is absolutely the season of physical preparation. I think that many of us have been content to hide behind our journals in this season, and now God is calling us out.

As Christians, we have heard so many messages on Esther. We've heard it declared through the halls of church after church that perhaps we were made for "such a time as this". But what if this really is the time? What if there is something on the season we are in now, where if we'll partner with it today it will bring us supernaturally closer to the plans He has waiting for us.

I believe that we've been in a holding pattern of "getting ready" for so long, that it's easy to miss that the gates have been raised, the gun has sounded and the race is on! I feel in ways that I have never felt before, that this is a go season.

And today I want to pray over those of you whose heart is beating quickly as you read these words. As well as those of you who are hesitating to respond to the gentle go that the Father is whispering over you. God, I thank you for the season you have placed us in. I thank you that you have called us forward for this specific time in history, and that today you are saying over us, "it's time to go". I thank you for strategy and resources coming together in this time. And I thank you that what in the natural should take a long time, is being expedited by your spirit. I release over your daughters today signs in the Earth to confirm what you have been whispering to their spirits. And I bind every bit of fear and hesitation and release the creativity of the Lord for God ideas, manifested through your daughters for the furthering of your Kingdom that have never before been seen.

"Love never fails"

Day 29: The "L" Word

Have you ever been in church and been exhorted by the leader to lift up worship and tell the Lord that you love Him? Of course, you have. Have you ever done it and been embarrassed or shameful because the words felt empty leaving your lips? It's OK to nod yes ... I can't see you.

It was months ago at church as our worship set was winding down. It had already been a really great time in the Lord and we hadn't even made it to the Word yet. Everyone was standing in this holy and quiet moment, when the worship leader encouraged us to sing out and tell the Lord that we loved Him. As I began to sing my own song I felt the gravity of the words I was saying, but not the depth of the emotion. As I stood there listening to the room fill with prayers and songs I began to wonder, what does it really mean to tell the Lord we love him?

I remember when my oldest daughter was discovering the art of rebellion. It was around Christmas time and she had taken one of my husband's childhood ornaments and shattered it on the floor. We got down on her level, knowing full well that she was aware of what she was doing. "Tell daddy you're sorry" …. Silence. "I said, tell daddy you are sorry" … more defiant silence. The next 30 minutes felt like hours. What had begun as "say sorry" had turned into a conversation that we could not back down from. Eventually our daughter blurted out the words in a crying mess, "I'm sorry, I'm sorry". We knew she could say sorry, but we questioned if she knew exactly what it meant.

Going back to this moment in church, I started thinking of my marriage with my husband. When we got married we expressed our love for each other, and we meant every word. But in that moment, there was no way we could know the extent of how that expression would be tested. Just like any other marriage as ours developed we learned more deeply about our confession. As a young couple, we experienced difficult and hurtful times just like anyone else. We learned what it meant to walk through hardship. Not only hardship that came at us as a unit, but also disappointment that was produced by one of us and endured by the other. Saying "I love you" had grown roots that reached far past the alter of our wedding day and wrapped around covenant.

As I stood in that moment of worship I felt a deep rush of love for the Father flow through me. My expression of love wasn't something I was giving in passing, on the surface of my emotions. It wasn't something that I could say, but like my daughter, couldn't fully grasp why. My "I love you" had become a declaration I could make because of the victories and failures, because of the joyful times as well as the disappointments, because through the sun and the storms the Lord had remained faithful to me.

In no way am I saying that everything has been perfect or even close to it. If you've read my story you might even think I'm crazy to love God the way I do. But when we search our hearts and reflect on our deepest moments of disappointment, the one person we can always find standing by is the Lord. Now that's not to say that we don't have actual people that have selflessly weathered our storms with us, but rather in those moments of our deepest thoughts, when we couldn't muster the energy or courage to express them to anyone else, the Lord was there, wrapping His covenant love around us. And I don't know about you, but that is a love I can't help but respond to.

Maybe today as you read this you know you have found yourself struggling with expressing your love to the Lord. Maybe something or things have happened that have thrown you off center and brought you into a place of questioning your affection for the Father and His affection for you. And today I believe the Lord is inviting you into an honest discourse with Him.

No one can love us as deeply as Jesus. And I hear Him saying in this moment that you don't have to hide your disappointments from Him, but rather you have permission to bring them to Him and allow His tender mercies to cover you. He was acquainted with our pain in every way, and I believe that today if you are willing to take a step forward that He wants to meet you in that place.

God, I pray for those struggling with their affections for you, and those who are questioning your affection for them. God rush over them in this moment. Show them that you truly are the God who stands in the fire with us and preserves us from the stench of the flames. I pray that today you would wrap the roots of your covenant love around your daughters, and choke out every lie that tries to cast a shadow on the true depth with which you love us. And I ask that today you give us a deeper revelation of the love You have for us, and just how far into our souls your reach can go. Restore the broken places of our heart and bring us into wholeness as we lift up our eyes to trust again in you.

> "Be in good health, just as your soul prospers"

Day 30: An Inside Job

Have you ever had a wound that was slow to heal? I have had my fair share.

A while back I was having a conversation with my sister-in-law. She is a homeschooling beast, and was telling me and a few other ladies about some reading she had been doing about how wounds heal. She was sharing it as an encouragement to one of our friends who was experiencing a really unfortunate relational issue with another woman. She was talking about the purpose of healing from the inside out, and how the body was designed this way to prevent the trapping of germs inside the body which would obviously cause more damage. It seemed like such a simple and obvious lesson, but in the moment, it was helping to unravel a healing that God was doing inside of a heart.

Several weeks after that conversation I had just come home from a small group meeting, with a heart that was exceptionally full. On top of my physical journey with multiple surgeries and facial paralysis, we were also in a new church home looking to develop relationships once again. And both seemed to be taking forever. That night I was reflecting on how faithful God had been to us in what seemed to be a season that would not end. As I was walking through the living room I glanced up at a mirror mounted on our wall. I was smiling, but for the first time since I could remember I didn't see paralysis or asymmetry, I just saw me. In that moment, Holy Spirit whispered, "this healing is an inside job".

3 John 1:2 says, "Beloved, I pray that all may go well with you and that you may be in good health, as it goes well with your soul." ESV

For me, the healing that was going on in my heart was directly connected to the healing that was taking place in my body. And in that moment the Lord was showing me that as I yielded to one, both would progress. Talk about motivation.

Have you ever had situations in your life that you felt were running parallel to one another? In your mind they didn't really intersect, other than the constant ping pong game you played going back and forth from one to another. But then, in a moment of revelation, God showed you just how intimately connected they really were.

I don't think it's a coincidence that John talks about the connection of our bodies to our souls in respect to prospering. I believe he had received by revelation what the world today is catching on to. And that is that the two are very connected.

For me in that moment it was the realization that the healing of my soul was fueling the healing of my body. And it is something I am continuing to learn in real time.

What is it for you? Is there something knotted up in your soul that is keeping you from a physical breakthrough? I am not saying that if you're sick it is because of a soul issue. But what I am saying, is that if the Bible stopped to emphasis the relation of the two, that we would be wise to take note. Like I said before, this is something I am currently walking out with the Lord. But I do believe that if we can start to put the puzzle pieces together, that there is a deeper healing in both our bodies and minds that we can experience.

    Today I want to pray for the prospering of your body as well as your soul. God, I speak your healing anointing over those who are sick in their bodies. I thank you that your payment on the cross left nothing undone. And I pray that our souls would line up with the truth that it is the joy of the Lord that truly becomes our strength. I declare today that wholeness would overtake your daughters, and that your revelation would shine on hearts and reveal places in this moment that need a touch from You. God, I thank you that you are good, and that you always lead us gently. And today I declare that inside jobs are becoming outside jobs. That women right now are being set free in the mind as well as body, and that you and you alone are the true reconciler of our lives. Thank you, Jesus for your Lordship over us. In You we never have to be afraid.

Thoughts and Prayers

Thoughts and Prayers

Thoughts and Prayers

Thoughts and Prayers

Thoughts and Prayers

Thoughts and Prayers